The British Television
Location Guide

The British Television Location Guide

Steve Clark and Shoba Vazirani

Contents

GREAT BRITAIN
Emmerdale
Spooks
Little Britain
Doctor Who
Life on Mars

The British Television Location Guide

Written by Steve Clark and Shoba Vazirani

First published in 2008 by Splendid Books Limited

Splendid Books Limited
PO Box 813
Portsmouth
Hampshire
PO1 9EY
www.splendidbooks.co.uk

British Library Cataloguing in Publication Data is available from The British Library

ISBN: 978 0 9558916 0 1

Designed by Design Image Ltd.
www.design-image.co.uk

Printed and bound by Borcombe SP, Romsey

Introduction

There can't be many of us who haven't at some point while watching a television series, thought: "I wonder where that was filmed?" Well, hopefully this book will solve many of those puzzles and help settle a few family arguments!

The British Television Location Guide can be enjoyed by those viewers who do their location spotting from their armchair or by the more adventurous who prefer to go out and visit some of the wonderful places they've seen on screen.

From the splendour of Lacock, the setting for *Cranford* to the streets of Bristol where many episodes of *Only Fools and Horses* were filmed, there's bound to be something for everyone.

Television companies go to great lengths to find perfect locations for their series and the places they choose aren't necessarily famous. Among them are some of the best-kept secrets of the British countryside and heritage, many well worth visiting.

While many of the locations and places featured in this book are open to the public, there are some that belong to private individuals. We're sure our readers will remember this and respect that these properties are out of bounds.

Obviously lots of the programmes we've covered are filmed in more than one location – often in different parts of the country - but we've listed them in the area where most of the filming took place or, in the case of classic *Doctor Who*, next to a companion section.

Finally, while every effort has been taken to check that all details contained in this book are correct at the time of going to press, readers may wish to confirm opening times before setting out on a long journey.

Happy location hunting!

Steve Clark and Shoba Vazirani

Location Map

Scotland

The North West

Jersey, Ireland and Northern Ireland

Wales

The South West

The North

The Midlands

East Anglia

London

The South East

The South West

Bonekickers

Bath

Set against the backdrop of the beautiful ancient city of Bath, *Bonekickers* follows a team of archaeologists as they delve into the past and unravel ancient mysteries which have relevance to the modern day. The group - played by actors Julie Graham, Hugh Bonneville, Adrian Lester and Gugu Mbatha-Raw – are based at the fictional Wessex University, although the campus of the real-life University of Bath was used for filming.

Where possible, filming took place during university holidays at the start of 2008 and at weekends so that students and lecturers were interrupted as little as possible. Some rooms in the city's other university, Bath Spa, were also used and doubled as an office in New York. The archaeology laboratory where the team works was created at the production offices, a disused telephone exchange on Granville Road, Lansdown. Two offices were knocked together and converted into a lab, archive and dry room which appear in every episode. Woods off Farleigh Rise, Bathford, were used to film an impressive fight scene where The Knights Templar are ambushed by the Saracens while Larkhall open ground became the ambush site in the present day. Overlooking the area is Larkhall Springs Nursing Home in which a dying patient is apparently cured when he touches a piece of the relic discovered in the dig site outside the nursing home. The historic Roman Baths in Abbey Church Yard were used for several scenes and the team can be seen exploring underneath the baths which are a popular tourist location. The famous Assembly Rooms in Bennett Street were converted into a museum in one episode. An invaluable artefact, an archway from Iraq was installed there by the set designers as well as a host of other objects. It was also the location for a major fight scene. The American Museum which is next door to Bath University, was also used in certain shots of the 'museum' scene.

Above: **The *Bonekickers* cast and crew filming at Brean Down, Burnham-on-Sea.**

Picturesque Brean Down in Burnham-on-Sea sees the archaeology team searching a cave. The location has spectacular views and was also used to shoot *Elizabeth: The Golden Age*, while Brean Beach was used to film the BBC's *Dracula*, starring Marc Warren. Stately home Chavenage just outside Tetbury where *Lark Rise to Candleford* was also filmed, was used in a number of scenes. The impressive grounds doubled up as 1917 Verdun Fields and were used for woods in another episode. Another stately home, Sheldon Manor, also featured as an Elizabethan house to where one of the characters is taken by kidnappers. Sheldon, which also appeared in Persuasion, is situated at Chippenham, Wiltshire and is one of county's oldest inhabited manor houses. See www.sheldonmanor.co.uk for details.

Sets were specially created at a disused hangar in Colerne Airfield in Wiltshire for the filming of special effects scenes which were supposedly underneath a 13th Century Dovecot in Herefordshire. In these scenes, the characters have a sword fight while swinging from ropes over burning crucifixes. A few more locations worth mentioning include the Georgian Bath Spa Hotel, used as hotel in which an Iraqi delegation stay in episode four. George Baynton Bookbinders in Manvers Street doubled up as an Ecclesiastical library in the opening episode and again in episode five as a library in modern day Verdun; the Tank Museum in Bovington, Dorset, was used for tank interior scenes set in 1917 and the historic Wells Cathedral in Somerset which retained its own identity.

The Camomile Lawn

Veryan

Fans of the 1992 Channel Four drama *The Camomile Lawn* will be delighted to know that they can actually stay at Broom Parc *(pictured right)*, the attractive Edwardian clifftop house used in the series, as Keith and Lindsay Righton who live there run it as a bed and breakfast.

Right: **Broom Parc has stunning views of the sea.**

When filming took place in 1991 Lindsay and Keith had already planned to open the house up as a bed and breakfast. By the time they opened for business the following year, *The Camomile Lawn* had been on television and newspapers had written about the house. The publicity helped the Rightons to start their business. "The timing couldn't have been better," said Lindsay. Very little had to be done to the outside of the house before filming of the series began but the interior had to be redecorated three times to reflect the different periods in the drama. Every time this happened the family had to move lock, stock and barrel up to the former servants' quarters on the top floor. After filming ended Channel Four redecorated the house to Keith and Lindsay's taste.

The house, which was built in 1908 and is actually owned by the National Trust, has wonderful views of the sea but Lindsay said it might not be everyone's ideal home when it gets stormy in the winter. "We're very happy here although other people may not wish to live right on the edge of a cliff in the teeth of a gale and the upkeep of the house is quite substantial. It's very exposed, so if the wind blows the central heating bill goes out of the window!" she added. For more details see: www.broomparc.co.uk

Casualty

Bristol

When *Casualty* launched in 1986, no one could have predicted it would become television's longest-running medical drama, pulling in millions of viewers and winning several awards. Set in the Holby City Hospital in the fictional city of Holby, the series is actually filmed in Bristol. Although this isn't mentioned on screen guest artists often have Bristolian accents and city landmarks are often to be glimpsed in many episodes.

For instance, the Clifton Suspension Bridge and the floating harbour have made quite a few appearances, both locations synonymous with Bristol and the South West. The majority of *Casualty* is shot at a specially-constructed set in an industrial warehouse in the St Phillips area of Bristol. It was decided early on, after the BBC's production team visited almost every hospital in Bristol, that trying to film a television series within a real-life working hospital simply wouldn't work.

At the time, they were really only looking for a hospital to shoot the exterior part of the hospital as it was always the case that the interiors should be filmed on a purpose built set. Even so, the thought of camera teams and actors getting in the way of real ambulance crews ferrying real casualties into hospital was a major concern. "None of the hospitals we looked at fitted the bill as access to them would have been very difficult because they were proper working hospitals," explained *Casualty* founder Producer, the late Geraint Morris, who also produced other hit shows including *The Onedin Line* and *Wycliffe* and who sadly passed away in 1997.

"Then someone said to me: 'I've passed an old orphanage that looks a bit like an old hospital, is it worth going to see?' I said: 'Let's give it a try,' so we went and had a look and when we got there I said, 'This is it!'" The site had not been used as an orphanage for many years and was in fact home to the Brunel College of Arts and Technology. The old grey stone buildings certainly looked the part for an old style hospital and fortunately, the college authorities agreed the BBC could use it for filming the outside of Holby City Hospital.

Casualty exterior shots were filmed there for 16 years until 2002, when a new exterior set was built at St Phillips close to the interior set, so now virtually all filming is in one location. "Various locations around the Bristol area are used for *Casualty* such as a number of houses which feature as characters' homes," explained Natalie Moore of Bristol Film Office. "They tend to use a lot of roads, particularly dual carriageways such as Hengrove Road which is surrounded by fields so you can't really tell where it is, to film stunts and so on.

"They also use the city centre and go to Clifton from time to time and occasionally roads have to be closed to enable filming to proceed or they have traffic control on smaller roads. Even though it's a long-running series, they still have to run everything past us and we make sure it can happen; I have to say, there are rarely any problems and things tend to run smoothly."

As *Casualty* has been running for so long, it's hardly surprising that literally hundreds of locations have been used over the years and the show's location managers are always on the look-out for new possibilities. Some time ago, the local paper, the Bristol Evening Post carried an advertisement for Bristol residents to offer up their properties for shooting.

Holby City

Borehamwood

Despite being a spin-off of *Casualty* and supposedly set in the same fictional hospital, *Holby City* is filmed nowhere near Bristol. It is actually shot entirely on a purpose-built set at Elstree Studios in Borehamwood, Hertfordshire, also home to *EastEnders*. An office block used by BBC staff is used as one of the hospital's entrances.

Occasionally, characters and storylines of the two series overlap and sometimes characters in one refer to a ward in another, but generally, the two series have separate identities.

Cranford

Lacock

It takes a pretty special television production to entice an Oscar-winning Hollywood actress to star but that's exactly what the BBC's 2007 dramatisation of the star-studded costume drama *Cranford* proved to be. Dame Judi Dench thrilled creator Sue Birtwistle when she agreed to take on the role of Miss Matty Jenkyns, whose hopes and rebellious spirit are crushed when she is forced as a young woman to give up the man she loves, played by Michael Gambon.

It was the first BBC role for the in-demand actress since she starred in the highly-acclaimed film about Queen Victoria, *Mrs Brown*, 10 years earlier. Other big names involved include Imelda Staunton, Francesca Annis, Philip Glenister, Julia Sawalha and Greg Wise, all of whom along with the wonderful costumes and of course superb locations, helped create a winning combination.

The five-part drama, set in a small Cheshire market town in the 1840s, was based on three novels by Elizabeth Gaskell: Cranford, My Lady Ludlow and Mr Harrison's Confessions and follows the small absurdities and major tragedies in the lives of the people of *Cranford*.

Ideally, the production team would have loved to use the town of Knutsford in Cheshire to film *Cranford*. This was Gaskell's original model. However the cost of disguising 21st

Below: **Turning back the clock - but Lacock didn't need too much work done to make it the perfect place to double as *Cranford*.**

Century modernisation proved too high and they had to look elsewhere to shoot. Eventually Lacock in Wiltshire, which has been used for the *Harry Potter* films and dramas including *Pride and Prejudice*, *Moll Flanders* and *Emma*, was chosen as it is owned by the National Trust and outwardly displays few trappings of modern living. Indeed, visitors to Lacock have remarked how wandering through the stunning village on the southern edge of the Cotswolds, is like stepping back into the 18th Century with its stone and thatched cottages and absence of road markings.

Because the National Trust looks after Lacock there are no telephone poles or television aerials in sight so there was no need for the production team to remove such 21st Century paraphernalia.

Above: (left) **Imelda Staunton as town gossip Miss Pole** *(centre and right)* **two views of *Cranford* sets where attention to detail was crucial in bringing the series to life** *Opposite page:* **Philip Glenister as Mr Carter.**

They just had to cover the ground to conceal the tarmac, hide various bits of front doors, redress windows and build the front of Johnson, *Cranford's* new store, over the front of the local pub. The village is within easy reach of Chippenham, Wiltshire by road and rail and boasts Lacock Abbey, a medieval cloistered abbey converted into the splendid country home of William Henry Fox Talbot who discovered the photographic process and the Fox Talbot Museum, where you can trace the history of photography.

In the centre of the village in the High Street is the 18th Century Red Lion Inn which was perfectly transformed into Johnson's Stores by the BBC where Miss Matty and Miss Deborah Jenkyns (Eileen Atkins) are regularly seen shopping. Assistant Manager Sarah Upton said the conversion of the comfortable Inn into 19th Century 'stores' was impressive and captivated villagers as they watched set designers and engineers construct a whole new 'front' to the building. "For about two weeks it was very dark inside the building because all the windows and doors were blocked so as not to let in or out any light during the filming process," she explained. "What was so clever was that once the new front was built, you could actually walk behind it into the Inn but no one would ever have known.

"All the door frames and windows frames were painted by the BBC and afterwards, they painted it all back to its original state. It was extremely impressive and professional. "Other buildings in the village were also used to double up as the butchers or dairies and I know some people were asked for use of their homes for various scenes. For about three weeks in April 2007 it was a lot of fun in Lacock!" These days the Red Lion Inn is an idyllic weekend getaway. For reservations telephone 01249 730456. Among the

other locations used, the National Trust's West Wycombe Park doubled as Lady Ludlow's home Hanbury Court. The 18th Century home of Sir Francis Dashwood, founder of the notorious Hellfire Club, is one of England's finest theatrical houses and with its lavish interiors, complete with fine painted ceilings, it has proved the perfect setting for other productions including *Vanity Fair* and *The Importance of Being Earnest*. West Wycombe Park is set in the pretty Chilterns village of West Wycombe in Buckinghamshire and it is well worth a visit just to glimpse the Rococo gardens with their ornamental lake, statues and exquisitely landscaped lawns. Telephone 01494 755571 for tour information.

While making the journey to West Wycombe, why not also pop along to the nearby village of Radnage, also within the Chilterns hills and easily accessible from junction 5 of the M40 motorway? Here you'll find the 13th Century-built St Mary's Church which was used in the serial as Cranford Church. The team filmed there for three days in early summer and while it brought a happy buzz to the village, it was an experience the inhabitants of Radnage have experienced many times before. In fact, Radnage is most notable as the location for the 1987 post-war film *A Month in the Country* starring Colin Firth and Kenneth Branagh as well as the film version of *The Avengers* in 1998 and the TV movie *The Mystery of Men* the following year. On the edge of the Chiltern Hills is the splendid Ashridge Estate, an area of open countryside and woodland belonging to the National Trust which was used to shoot *Cranford*'s May Day scenes, while many of the stunning garden shots were obtained at the Trust's Winkworth Arboretum at Godalming in Surrey. Telephone 01494 755557 for further information on Ashridge and 01483 208252 for opening arrangements at the Arboretum.

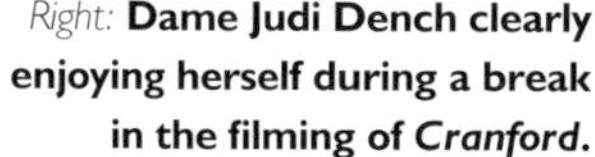

Right: **Dame Judi Dench clearly enjoying herself during a break in the filming of *Cranford*.**

Doc Martin

Port Isaac

Picturesque Port Isaac on the north Cornwall coast has always been a favourite destination for tourists but now it has extra appeal thanks to the success of ITV's hit drama series *Doc Martin*. The village was originally used as the setting for the 2000 feature film *Saving Grace* which starred Brenda Blethyn as a green-fingered widow who after discovering her late husband has left her with big debts, starts growing marijuana to make money. Martin Clunes co-starred as the local GP.

A year later Sky Pictures decided to make two spin-off films called *Doc Martin* and *Doc Martin and The Legend of The Cloutie* but plans for more films were then put on ice when Sky Pictures shut down in June 2001. But *Doc Martin* was destined to be seen again and in 2004 filming began on *Doc Martin*, in which the doctor, now called Dr Martin Ellingham, had been a high flying London surgeon but who had to give it up after developing a phobia of blood. When the local GP in the sleepy Cornish hamlet of Portwenn, where Ellingham spent his childhood holidays, dies, he decides to apply for the job, but the move to the country fails to improve his appalling bedside manner. He doesn't fit in easily as the locals were used to having a friendly GP to talk to and one who would write out a prescription at the drop of a hat. They get a shock when *Doc Martin* arrives because he couldn't be more curmudgeonly.

Below: **A view of Port Isaac over the rooftops.**

"Martin Ellingham might be a clever man in some ways, but he is completely stupid when it comes to dealing with people," said Martin Clunes. "They confound and confuse him. His people skills are terrible and he knows he's like it. He is just useless at small-talk and he's not used to talking to his patients as in his previous job they'd be out cold when he met them ready for him to operate on them."

Above: (left) **Doc Martin's house, Fern Cottage** *(centre)* **The Old School House Hotel that is used as Louisa's school and** *(right)* **the narrow streets in the village make driving tricky.**
Opposite page: **Martin Clunes and Caroline Catz pictured during a break in filming in Port Isaac.**

Port Isaac is a fabulous place and most of the village has been seen in *Doc Martin* at some point. Most notable to location hunters is Fern Cottage, which was *Doc Martin*'s surgery in the series up on the left on Roscarrock Hill. The building is clearly visible from pretty much everywhere in Port Isaac, but remember - it is a private house and only the exterior is used for filming (interior scenes are filmed at a studio) and there is a sign in the garden requesting that people do not peer through the windows.

At the bottom of Roscarrock Hill and best viewed from the other side of the harbour – is the stunning waterside house that was used as Bert's place. Directly opposite, on the other side of the harbour is the Old School Hotel and Restaurant www.theoldschoolhotel.co.uk the village's former school which is now a hotel but doubles as Portwenn School in the series, run by headmistress Louisa Glasson (Caroline Catz) whose will-they, won't-they relationship with the Doctor keeps viewers intrigued. Nearby is the Boathouse Stores which has appeared in the show and a few doors up from the hotel is Louisa's cottage.

The roads in Port Isaac are very narrow and you might want to consider parking at the top of the hill and walking down to the harbour. If you do decide to venture down by car then, if the tide is out, you can park on the beach – but keep an eye on the water level!

There are plenty of decent places to eat with everything from a cup of tea to a full culinary experience on offer. Among the places to eat is Golden Lion pub, which doubled as The Crab and Lobster in *Doc Martin* and nearby, in Middle Street, is the building that doubles as the chemist shop.

Royal National
Lifeboat
Institution
the
HOTEL
&
RESTAURANT

Harbour Lights

West Bay

At the beginning of 1999 the small Dorset village of West Bay was bracing itself for an influx of visitors anxious to catch a glimpse of the real-life setting for the BBC drama *Harbour Lights*. The show stars Nick Berry as small town harbourmaster Mike Nicholl, an ex-Royal Navy Lieutenant Commander. BBC bosses hoped his pulling power would bring the series the same sort of popularity that he'd achieved on ITV's *Heartbeat*. Sadly it didn't and it ended after two series.

Nicholl is in charge of the harbour of a small south coast town called Bridehaven where feuding families, ruthless business dealings and the sea dominate the lives of the people who work and play there. The quaint real-life 16th Century Bridport Arms Hotel, close to the sea, was one of the show's key locations and actually played two different places in the series. It offers accommodation - see: www.bridportarms.co.uk for details. When the BBC arrived they removed the bricks from the bricked up window of the landlord's bottle store outside, put in new frames, built a false porch on the front and changed the door. It then looked just like a cottage and played the entrance to Mike Nicholls' fictional home. The door opened but only led to a small hallway. Nearby is the Harbour Café which was run by music-loving Elvis. The on-screen harbourmaster's office is over the other side of the harbour and the exterior used for filming although interior scenes were usually shot elsewhere to avoid disrupting the work of the real harbourmaster.

The House of Eliott

Bristol

Modern day Bristol played 1920s London for the BBC's drama *The House of Eliott*. The city was chosen to double as the capital because it was easier and cheaper to film outside London and the houses in parts of Bristol fitted the bill. The exterior of Beatrice and Evengeline's (Louise Lombard and Stella Gonet, *pictured left*) *House of Eliott* design studio was filmed at number 24 Berkeley Square. When the BBC arrived they had to remove all traces of the 1990s to recreate London of the 1920s. Yellow lines were covered up with either latex paint or special mats which looked like cobblestones and the tops of parking meters were removed. Modern intercom systems on the outside of many of the buildings were usually disguised as old-fashioned doorplates. The Bristol branch of Coutts, in Corn Street, was used as fictional Gillespie Saroyan Bank and Clifton Girls School played home to Jack's apartment. The Wills Memorial Building at Bristol University, also played the interior of the Houses of Parliament and the former Will's Cigarette Factory was used as Jack's film studio. Royal Fort House in Royal Fort Gardens, played the offices of a rival fashion house, Hauseurs. Clifton Hill House, a university hall of residence, was used for a dinner party scene and the Orangery at another hall of residence, Goldney House, doubled as a teashop. Just across the River Avon at Leigh Woods is Leigh Court, a former mental hospital, which was used on the programme to play the interior of the Houses of Parliament, the interior of Buckingham Palace and the foyer of the Ritz Hotel. The impressive Pump Room in Cheltenham was used for several fashion shows and the bandstand outside was also used. The Assembly Rooms in Bath were used, first as an auction room, and later for a charity ball. The Guildhall was used for a charity concert and the City's Royal Victoria Park doubled as Hyde Park.

Lark Rise to Candleford

Tetbury

This charming and heart-warming drama was shot in 2007 and screened by the BBC the following year, much to the delight of Sunday evening viewers. Flora Thompson's autobiographical novel *Lark Rise to Candleford* was beautifully adapted by Bill Gallagher and won critical acclaim for its stunning depiction of the English countryside.

The 10-part drama is set in Lark Rise, a small Oxfordshire hamlet and the neighbouring market town of Candleford and examines the lives of workers and gentry as the 19th Century draws to a close. Their everyday comings and goings and concerns are seen through the eyes of Laura Timmins, played by actress Olivia Hallinan, who moves from Lark Rise to the wealthier Candleford to begin a new life, working for her mother's cousin Dorcas (Julia Sawalha) at the local post office.

Although set in Oxfordshire, *Lark Rise* which also stars Dawn French and Ben Miles, was actually filmed in and around Wiltshire, both at specially built studios and more prominently, at the stunning Chavenage House (*pictured below*) which doubled up as Sir Timothy Midwinter's home Candleford Manor. Both interiors and exteriors were shot extensively at Chavenage which is in Tetbury, not far from Prince Charles' home Highgrove, taking full advantage of its beautiful gardens outside and, its oak-floored, exquisitely decorated rooms inside which are steeped in history.

Below: **Beautiful Chavenage, one of the main locations for *Lark Rise to Candleford*.**

Originally built in 1538, there have been additions and renovations to the property over the centuries. Since Tudor times, only two families have owned Chavenage, the current owner David Lowsley-Williams having inherited the house from his uncle in 1958. These days, the property is very much a family home and even though it is open to the public on a part-time basis and incidentally, the perfect wedding venue, members of the Lowsley-Williams clan are never far away.

Above: **Dawn French with some young friends at Chavenage, one of the main locations for *Lark Rise to Candleford.***

David and his wife Rona have three children – George, Caroline and Katie - and six grandchildren who enjoy running around the 1800-acre estate with their dogs and riding their ponies. Caroline organises weddings – bookings have already been taken for years ahead - corporate events and of course filming at the house and she said the family were delighted when the BBC approached them to shoot Lark Rise at their home.

While it wasn't the first time Chavenage was used as a film location – an episode of ITV's *Poirot* was shot there as was part of the 2008 BBC series *Bonekickers*, an episode of BBC medical drama *Casualty* and *Grace and Favour,* an early 1990s follow-up to *Are You Being Served?* – it was the first time the house was featured so heavily in a major television drama.

"The location manager's brief was to find unspoiled countryside close to a manor house which was a difficult search," explained Caroline who enjoyed an idyllic childhood growing up in the ancestral home. "I showed her round Chavenage and although she'd been here before, it was as though a light bulb went off in her head."

Not only is the house made of limestone which is in keeping with the description of Candleford Manor, but do a 360 degree turn outside and nothing that wasn't there before 1881 such as electricity pylons and telephone cables, comes into view, which is perfect for a filming a drama set in the 19th Century.

Filming began in the early summer of 2007 but a particularly rainy season meant that certain scenes had to be shot again two or three months later. For instance, an area of picturesque garden set for a relaxing picnic turned into a lake as storms battered the south west. Also, an outbreak of foot and mouth disease meant that no pigs were available for the farm scenes.

Fans of *Lark Rise to Candleford* will recognise many of the rooms used if they visit Chavenage such as the Oakroom which doubled up as Lady Adelaide's drawing room, the anteroom which served as Sir Timothy's office and the ballroom which became the dining room in the series. As to be expected, the BBC asked to make certain alterations to the premises before shooting could commence and the Lowsley-Williams agreed.

"A big change was the gravel on the driveway which was blue granite originally but had to be limestone for the BBC's use," Caroline revealed. "So we had our gravel taken out and theirs put in which has stayed since. We like it very much actually! What I was most happy about though were the rubber mats the BBC gave us because the new gravel was very dusty at first. They have come in very useful!

"There are security lights outside the house which had to be covered up for filming purposes but they had to be uncovered every night for insurance reasons. So they made little polystyrene 'hats' which could be put on and off easily.

"Also, they gave us two standard lamps. Some of the lights in one of the rooms had to be removed and covered up with panelling because obviously the series is set in pre-electric times. So they very kindly gave us the lamps instead."

Other 'gifts' presented to the family by way of a thank you for the use of their beautiful home included a beech tree with a plaque commemorating the filming of *Lark Rise to Candleford* at Chavenage and two original sketches of costumes by the costume designer. These have been framed and are on display for visitors to enjoy.

If you're wondering where most of the village scenes were shot, these were filmed at a Grade II listed farm at Box, five miles east of Bath where a temporary village was specially created. Nearby Neston Park in Corsham with its beautiful historical buildings was also used as a backdrop for much of the series and a vast warehouse in Yate, 12 miles north east of Bristol was transformed into no fewer than 16 sets of many of the villages' interior scenes.

Caroline said the cast and crew of *Lark Rise* became friends of the family and they were often invited to join the production for meals. "We've grown up with having an open house and coming out of the loo to find a member of the public standing there is quite common," she chuckled.

Above: **Olivia Hallinan (Laura Timmins) pictured during a break in filming.**

"It was enormous fun having a film crew at the house and while our wedding guests were a bit concerned sometimes that their big day might be overshadowed – that never happened – visitors were always delighted to find a star or two in their midst. I remember Ben Miles was particularly popular and when he came out and gave a tourist a peck on the cheek she was thrilled." For further details about Chavenage House telephone 01666 502329 or see www.chavenage.com

Mistresses

Bristol

The tangled love lives of four 30-something modern women, all glamorous and successful in their own right, made Ecosse Films' drama for the BBC, *Mistresses*, unmissable week-night television. While the glossy series could have been filmed anywhere, it is actually the more glamorous locations of Bristol that were chosen to shoot the six-parter which stars Sarah Parish as GP Katie, Shelley Conn as party planner Jessica, Orla Brady as lawyer Siobhan and Sharon Small as 9/11 widow and mum of two Trudi. "We filmed all over Bristol," said Location Manager Rikke Dakin. "The idea was to make it look very glossy; we were after aspirational cafe society and the city proved to be perfect for our needs. We just wanted it all to look very cosmopolitan and hopefully, everyone will agree that it does."

Bristol University featured in a variety of sequences. For instance, its Senate Room doubled up as the GMC (General Medical Council) building which fans will remember is where GP Katie is quizzed about allegations of misconduct. A stylish restaurant scene was also shot in another building, filming taking place just after the university's students graduated in the summer of 2007. The big finale sequence where Trudi shops her lying husband to the police took place in At Bristol, a hands-on science tourist attraction at trendy Millennium Square in the centre of the city. For further information on this popular venue, go to www.at-bristol.org.uk In fact Millennium Square with its ultra-modern look and in close proximity to the redeveloped dockside, was the perfect backdrop for several scenes, fitting perfectly with the overall glamorous look of the show.

The characters are frequently seen dining in trendy restaurants and meeting in hotels and for these scenes, real eateries and hotels were often used. These include Bordeaux Quay on Canons Road, a popular harbour-side venue complete with brasserie, restaurant and deli all under one roof. Another is The Olive Shed at Princes Wharf, a river-front restaurant. Viewers may also recognise the stylish Hotel du Vin where Katie arranges to meet Sam (actor Max Brown) and where some of the rooms were used for interior shots. Other places of interest featured include the historic and stunning Blaise Castle Estate which boasts a small gothic castle dating back to the 18th Century called the Folly. It was here that a lesbian wedding that Jessica arranged took place. The Folly is now a ruin and open to the public on certain days during the summer only. For more information on the Estate contact the Estate Office on 0117 353 2268.

"Another place open to the public is the Architecture Centre, a very interesting little venue we used to stage an exhibition where Katie tries to inspire Sam when he says he doesn't want to go back to university," said Rikke. "We did it using models from Bristol University's architectural department so we got them all involved which was good." The Architecture Centre is located at Narrow Quay. For more information, go to www.architecturecentre.co.uk The youngsters of Clifton Primary School also got a chance to get involved in the drama when they were invited to become extras. As Trudi and her lover Richard (Patrick Baladi) both have young children, the two are often seen dropping off and picking up at the school gates. In case you were wondering if all those beautiful homes lived in by the characters are real or specially-built sets, they are actual homes around Bristol rented out by their owners.

The Onedin Line

Dartmouth

Anyone who visited the pretty town of Dartmouth in Devon during certain periods of the 1970s must have thought they had walked through a time tunnel. For the clock was turned back on much of the town and surrounding areas while the BBC filmed its popular period drama *The Onedin Line*. The drama, which was set in the 1860s, follows the life of James Onedin, played by Peter Gilmore with side-whiskers, as he runs his shipping line. Originally Liverpool was to have been used to film the series but the BBC turned to the West Country because they wanted to use the Devon based three-masted schooner The Charlotte Rhodes as their main sailing ship.

Right: **Bayard's Cove in Dartmouth, a key location for *The Onedin Line*.**

In a 1971 booklet on the programme Producer Peter Graham Scott, explained why he chose Dartmouth to play 19th Century Liverpool. "Architecturally the town had much to offer," he wrote. "With an authentic Victorian quay at Bayard's Cove, a functional Market Square, another fine quay at Kingswear, and many narrow streets, alleys and warehouses." Bayard's Cove, which hasn't really changed at all since filming, includes the old Customs House and The Dartmouth Arms, which was featured in several episodes. Scenes set in foreign countries were very common in the series - but in reality they were always filmed just round the corner. Bayard's Cove Fort, which was built in 1509, was used for an Arabian market scene, the outside of the George and Dragon in Clarence Street was in another Arabian episode and a Chinese scene was filmed in Avenue Gardens.

Across the river Dart, the quay at Kingswear doubled as Wilmington in the United States and the Maltster's Arms at Tuckenhay was used as a sailmaker's yard in Australia. Also in Tuckenhay is the old paper mill which was used for a fire sequence. The mill still stands but has now been converted into holiday homes. The River Dart itself was even used to play the upper reaches of the River Amazon when the crew of the Charlotte Rhodes were seen heading up it in canoes. Other locations in Dartmouth that were also used for filming include St Saviour's Church, where James and Anne get married, the historic market place and the Dartmouth Pottery which became a chandlery and a toffee shop. Outside Dartmouth, the basin at Exeter was used frequently for scenes involving ships unloading by big warehouses until a bridge built for the new M5 motorway in the mid 1970s brought use of the location to a halt as it was too low for the tall ships used for the series.

One Foot in the Grave

Christchurch

There were probably real cries of "I Don't Believe It" in sleepy Tresillian Way, a small street in the village of Walkford near Christchurch in Dorset during the 1990s. For as the real life setting for David Renwick's hit comedy series *One Foot In The Grave* some very strange things happened. Like 263 garden gnomes being delivered to the front lawn of poor old Victor Meldrew or an old Citroen being dumped in his skip. Life for Victor (Richard Wilson) is rather testing a lot of the time and that in turn doesn't make things very easy for his long-suffering wife Margaret.

The series ran from 1990 until 2000 and when Victor finally ends up in a grave after falling victim to a hit and run driver, fans made sure he wasn't forgotten. In fact floral tributes were laid near a railway bridge at Shawford near Winchester near to the spot where Victor met his end. Richard Wilson told the local paper, the *Hampshire Chronicle,* that Shawford was "the perfect place" for Victor to end his days. "I can't give anything away, but I can see why we've come here. It's very picturesque," he said

Below: (left) **Tresillian Way, Walkford** *(centre)* **tributes to Victor** *(right)* **Victor and Margaret.**

Only Fools and Horses

Bristol

It's no real wonder that the long arm of the law has never quite managed to catch up with dodgy dealing Del Boy Trotter. For if the boys in blue have been looking for Del in his manor of Peckham they've been looking in the wrong place. *Only Fools And Horses* – which stars David Jason as wheeler-dealer Del Boy Trotter and Nicholas Lyndhurst as his dopey brother Rodney – became increasingly rarely shot in London - and has never actually been shot in Peckham. It used to be filmed in and around the capital until it became too popular on screen and the crowds who gathered to watch filming grew too large. "Filming in London was a pain in the neck and we used to lose a lot of filming," said Ray Butt, the show's first producer. "I remember filming in Chapel Street in London and the crowds used to come round but they wouldn't be quiet and usually we'd have to stop during school breaks. It just became impossible to work."

Originally lots of London locations were used including Hammersmith cemetery, where Granddad's funeral takes place, in *Strained Relations*, The Alma pub at the corner of Chapel Market and Baron Street in Islington which is seen in *It Never Rains* and *Diamonds Are For Heather* and Hanwell Community Centre Westcott Crescent, London, which was in *Cash and Curry*. Witley Gardens, Southall Green, was the street in *Ashes to Ashes*, where Trigger's grandfather's urn is sucked up by a passing road sweeper lorry and Ravenscourt Park in Hammersmith in the episode *As One Door Closes*. Outside London, Butser Hill, near Petersfield, Hampshire was used for the hang gliding scene in *Tea For Three* and the Duke of Malebury's stately home in *A Royal Flush* was Clarendon Park, Wiltshire, but it isn't open to the public.

The series began to be filmed all round the country and there has been a Nag's Head in Hull, Ipswich, Brighton, London and Bristol and a Peckham street market in Hull, Ipswich, Bristol and Salisbury. As Ray Butt said: "You can set up a street market anywhere. All you need is a long run of walls and then put some stalls out." Bristol though became the most regularly used setting for the show. "Architecturally it had everything we needed in terms of pubs, houses and a market and most importantly we found the right block of flats," said producer Gareth Gwenlan. So instead of Harlech Tower, Park Road East, Acton, London, the original setting, Whitemead House, in Duckmoor Road, Bristol became Nelson Mandela House for the duration of filming and residents got used to seeing Del's dodgy yellow three-wheeler parked nearby.

From then on, lots of Bristol was used for filming the show including: In *Dates*, Bristol North Baths, Gloucester Road, which was the police station, 46 Old Market Street, which was the dating agency, and The White House, West Street, Bedminster www.whitehorsebedminster.co.uk which was the Nag's Head, 187 Gloucester Road, now Planet Pizza, was where Trigger takes a date and Shellard Road in Filton was where Rodney jumps a red light while trying to impress nervous Nerys. London also featured briefly - the Trotter van flying over a bridge was shot at Talbot Road, Isleworth and Del and Raquel meet under the clock at Waterloo Station. The Old Granary, Charlotte Street, which appeared in *Yuppy*

Left: **David Jason and Nicholas Lyndhurst share a joke doing the filming of *Only Fools and Horses*.**

Above: (top) **David Jason and Nicholas Lyndhurst take a break while filming *Only Fools and Horses* outside** *(bottom)* **Whitemead House** *Opposite page:* **Del and Rodney do a runner.**

Love, where it was the exterior location of the basement wine bar where Del famously falls over, also played a casino in *Fatal Extraction,* is now a Loch Fyne restaurant. Across the road at 46-48 Charles Fox House was the location of Rodney's adult education class. The Parkside Night Club, Bath Road, 10-16 York Street, (which was used as Alan Parry's business), flats at Guild Court, Redcliffe Back and the Boardwalk Shopping Centre were all used in *Rodney Come Home*. Henry's Hothouse, Whiteladies Road and Shoots floating restaurant were both used for *The Chance of a Lunchtime* and Raquel's audition in *Stage Fright* took place at the Courage Social Club in Willway Road.

The Conservatory Bar at Arnos Manor Hotel on Bath Road in Bristol was used in *Danger UXD* in the scene where Rodney takes Cassandra to dinner. The hotel was also the venue for disco scenes in *Yuppy Love* and *Rodney Come Home*. The rear of Arnos Manor Hotel in Bath Road was used in *Chain Gang* as the One Eleven Club. Lockside Cafe on Brunel Lock Road, Bristol was the location for Sid's Cafe in the 1993 Xmas Special *Fatal Extraction* and the 1996 episodes *Heroes and Villains* and *Modern Men*. Back then it was a greasy spoon, but now, according to its website www.lockside.net, it is a 'polished spoon.' A car showroom on Marsh Road was the location for Boycie's car showroom in *Time on our Hands* and Bristol City's car park at Ashton Gate was used for a market in *Fatal Extraction, Heroes and Villains*, and *Strangers on the Shore*. But Bristol didn't have a monopoly on filming. For example, The Benbom Brothers' funfair at Margate, the Roman Galley pub in Thanet Way, Canterbury and the forecourt of Margate railway station were all used for the episode *The Jolly Boys' Outing* and Tandoori Nights, King Street, London appeared in *Chain Gang*. It was back to London for scenes of Del and Rodney searching for Albert in *He Ain't Heavy, He's My Uncle* and the following places were used: Tower Bridge, HMS Belfast, Portobello Green, Acklam Road East, Malton Road and Portobello Road Market. The airport used in *The Sky's The Limit* was Stansted,

The hilarious scene when Raquel gives birth to Damian Trotter was supposed to be in Peckham but was actually filmed at the maternity wing of Hillingdon Hospital in Uxbridge in the episode *Three Men, a Woman and a Baby.* The scenes of Damian's christening in *Miami Twice: The American Dream* were actually filmed at two different churches. The interior scenes were filmed at St John's Church in Ladbroke Grove and the outside shots were done at St John's Church in Kentish Town. The Nag's Head used for the 1992 Christmas special *Mother Nature's Son* was the White Admiral Pub at Lover Bevendean in Brighton, not far from the allotments in Natal Road which were used as Grandad's old allotment in Peckham. The area in front of Whitemead House, Bristol, was used for the riot scene in *Fatal Extraction.* It was back to Bristol for the famous Batman and Robin scene in *Heroes and Villains* which was filmed at the shopping centre at The Horsefair in Broadmead and Rodney chases a yob past shops in Oxford Street and also down Nottingham Street and Hill Avenue in the same episode. The Harrison watch was found at Del's garage, a stone's throw from Whitemead House and when the Trotters sell it in *Time on Our Hands*, the auction scenes were filmed at Sotheby's, 34-35 New Bond Street, London. Marine Parade, Woodland Road, and the Dragon Kiss restaurant in Regent Street, Weston-Super-Mare all appeared in *If They Could See Us Now* and if you fancy a trip abroad, Del and Rodney take a ferry from Portsmouth to represent Albert at a ceremony in France, scenes for which were filmed in Gatteville-le-Phare in France. Finally, in the last episode *Sleepless in Peckham,* Greenbank Cemetery in Greenbank Road, Bristol was used for a moving scene where Rodney and Del visit their Mum's grave.

Persuasion

Bath

Beautiful and historical Bath featured heavily in ITV's stunning adaptation of Jane Austen's *Persuasion* which was filmed in 2006 and screened the following year to critical acclaim. It is of course a city close to Jane Austen's heart as she lived there in the early 1800s and chose it as the setting for both *Northanger Abbey* and *Persuasion*. This version starred Rupert Penry-Jones as Captain Wentworth and Sally Hawkins as Anne Elliot, an 'old maid' of 27 living a quiet life with her noble family in their country manor home, Kellynch Hall until events force a change on the whole family, particularly Anne. "We tried to base as much of Persuasion as we could in Bath but there were some locations we had to travel outside the city for," explained Location Manager Fiona Frankham. "But even then, we tried to stay as close to the area as we could. We filmed beach scenes at Lyme Regis in Dorset on the Cobb which was great. We also filmed at Golden Cap, five miles east of Lyme Regis."

Stunning Sheldon Manor in Chippenham doubled as Uppercross Hall to where Anne decamps after her family are forced to leave Kellynch. One of the oldest inhabited manor houses in Wiltshire with sections dating back to the 13th Century, the property boasts glorious gardens making it an idyllic wedding – and of course filming – location. The house

Above: **Bath Street in Bath - used for a market scene in ITV's 2006 version of *Persuasion*.**

is open to the public and can be hired out for special functions. See www.sheldonmanor.co.uk for details. The Coaching Inn which was supposedly at Lyme was actually shot at Great Chalfield Manor, near Melksham in Wiltshire. Chalfield is looked after by the National Trust and is renowned for its gardens. Indeed these were filmed extensively for scenes of Anne and her cousins out walking. Telephone 01225 782239 to find out about opening times or see www.nationaltrust.org.uk The interior of Camden Place, the Bath property the Elliott family head to after leasing out Kellynch, was actually Neston Park in Corsham and the exterior was Number One Royal Crescent in the centre of Bath. Neston Park is a country estate owned by the Fuller family (as in Fuller's London Pride ale), built in 1790. In case you were wondering, the elegant and stately Kellynch itself was filmed at a private house, the owners of which prefer not to make public. If you visit Bath make sure you find time to visit The Pump Room, which is referred to in the novel and used accordingly on television. "No major changes had to be made inside the Pump Room, although of course it was emptied for filming purposes," said Jenni Wagstaffe of Bath Film Office. "It was a delight to behold as filming brought to life a scene straight out of Austen's day." The National Trust-owned Assembly Rooms in Bennett Street were used to stage a concert where Captain Wentworth sees Anne and leaves. The rooms are home to the Fashion Museum and are available to hire for special events. Go to www.nationaltrust.org.uk to find out more. Bennett Street itself was also used as the address of Mrs Smith and Westgate Buildings. It also doubled as Queens Square, which itself was too small to close down for filming purposes. Royal Crescent became Camden Place to where Anne's father and sister move when they leave Kellynch and the romantic final scene where Anne and Wentworth kiss at the end of *Persuasion* was also shot there.

Above: **Rupert Penry-Jones and Sally Hawkins pictured during a break in the filming of *Persuasion*.**

The beautiful Botanical Gardens in Royal Victoria Park became the exterior of Queens Square which again was unsuitable for filming on that particular day. Nearby Western Road was closed during shooting to minimise noise. The very narrow cobbled Queen Street was used on another day for a scene in which Wentworth is searching for Anne. He looks in an art shop window and so a shop was specially dressed for the purpose. "As it's a very narrow street, it wasn't easy to film there and it took a lot of effort with marshals keeping everyone back and making sure everything was just so when suddenly this cyclist appeared and decided to disregard everybody and cycle all the way through the shot!" Jenni recalled. "You should have seen the expression on his face when he realised he was in the middle of this period scene." The final day of filming took place at Green Park where Anne and Wentworth finally admit their feelings to each other. Grand Parade was also used for one of these closing scenes, along with Bath Street. The latter was transformed into a spectacular period market which was all the more amazing considering it is one of the busiest streets in the city centre, being as it is in close proximity to the ever popular Roman Baths.

The 1995 version of *Persuasion* was arguably the BBC's finest adaptation of a Jane Austen novel by virtue of Director Roger Michell's deliberately dowdy costumes and settings, making it altogether less glossy than other Austen dramatisations. Much was filmed in Bath with both the Assembly Rooms and Pump Room being used for some scenes including a concert. The nearby Abbey Churchyard also featured as did 13 Old Bond Street, now a Starbucks coffee shop, which coincidentally played a teashop. A private house at 94 Sydney Place was used as several different screen settings. Outside Bath beautiful Sheldon Manor at Chippenham, the surviving manor house of a long gone mediaeval village, also appeared in this version doubling as The Musgrove's home. Barnsley House at Barnsley near Cirencester in Gloucestershire, played Kellynch Hall in *Persuasion* and is now a hotel and wedding venue. See www.barnsleyhouse.com for details.

Poldark

Cornwall

Cornwall was the setting for *Poldark*, the BBC's swashbuckling saga about heroic war veteran Ross Poldark, played by Robin Ellis. Set in the 18th Century the series was a huge hit with viewers both in Britain and around the world, who revelled in the stories of tin mining, smuggling and skulduggery. Ross and his wife Demelza, played by Angharad Rees live at Nampara, which is actually a stone farmhouse, Botallack Manor. Other scenes at Nampara were filmed at nearby Pendeen Manor. Ross' cousin Francis and his wife Elizabeth, live at Trenwith. In the first series Trenwith was played by Tudor Godolphin House at Godolphin Cross. Godolphin, which is now owned by the National Trust, was used when Trenwith is sacked and burnt, when Trenwith is attacked by miners and scenes where Ross Poldark first meets Demelza at the Redruth Fair were filmed in the grounds.

Doctor Dwight Enys' home in the series was actually Doyden Castle, a gothic folly built in the 19th Century. The folly, at Port Quin in north Cornwall, is high up on the cliffs and has spectacular views. It can be rented from the National Trust. Not far from Port Quin, at Trebetherick, is Enodoc Church which was used for the wedding of Francis and Elizabeth. Another church, Towednack, was used for Francis' father's funeral. Lots of filming took place on the north coast from Botallack in the far west to the River Camel where Padstow stands, in the Penzance area, Prussia Cove, and on the south coast at Charlestown, which was also used for the 1998 ITV drama *Frenchman's Creek*. Cornwall also doubled for France with part of the Fowey estuary, near Lerryn Creek playing a landing point for Ross and his friends in their bid to free Doctor Enys from French prison Fort Baton. St Mawes Castle, an English Heritage property, at the entrance to Falmouth played the fort. See www.english-heritage.org.uk for further details.

Below: **Stunning St Mawes Castle in Falmouth, doubled as a French fort in *Poldark*.**

Sense and Sensibility

Bideford

Anyone familiar with the stunning coastal walkway between Hartland Quay and Hartland Point which is to be found on the Hartland Abbey Estate near Bideford, north Devon may well have recognised it while watching the BBC's superb adaptation of Jane Austen's *Sense and Sensibility.* It was here that much of the three-part serialisation starring such names as David Morrissey and Janet McTeer was filmed during an often wet May 2007. The Estate which has been classified as an area of outstanding natural beauty is owned by Sir Hugh and Lady Angela Stucley and tucked away in a sheltered valley is Blackpool Mill Cottage which was heavily featured in the drama, as Barton Cottage.

It was to here that the Dashwood Family – sisters Elinor (Hattie Morahan) and Marianne (Charity Wakefield) - decamp upon the death of their father, along with their widowed mother (McTeer) and begin to build themselves a new life. But the cottage seen in the drama looks somewhat different to the actual building used thanks to the skills of the BBC's set designers, as Lady Stucley explained: "They added dormer windows to the roof of the cottage, shutters and a porch which actually didn't go anywhere. The actors were seen stepping inside but it was just a front. They also added a chimney to the sea end of the property so they had three chimneys instead of the two that are normally there."

Right: **Picturesque Blackpool Mill Cottage used as Barton Cottage in *Sense and Sensibility.***

The BBC also obtained the family's permission to paint the cottage and of course returned it to its natural state once filming was over. A year earlier, German TV used it as it was to film Rosamunde Pilcher's *The Shell Seekers*, choosing not to make any external alterations.

If you fancy staying at Blackpool Mill cottage, it is available for rent for up to eight persons although as you can imagine it is booked up well in advance. See www.hartlandabbey.com for details. "It was always popular with regulars but now we're absolutely inundated," added Lady Stucley.

The Studleys themselves live in Hartland Abbey which has been in their family since it was handed to them by Henry VIII. A stunning building, it is the obvious choice for many a location manager as is the five miles of coastline which belongs to the family. In 2004, a supernatural thriller, *The Dark*, was shot here as well as the BBC's *A Natural History of Britain* with Alan Titchmarsh a year earlier. The fabulous coastline even doubled up as the Caribbean island of St Lucia in the Michael Caine movie *Water*. "We're used to having camera crews filming in our midst," Lady Stucley continued. "The grounds of Hartland Abbey were used as a production base for *Sense and Sensibility* and it was great fun having actors wandering about in costumes eating ice-creams and mingling with everyone. It was wonderful to see coachmen with their gleaming carriages pulled by beautiful horses." In fact, in some scenes part of the grounds of the Abbey were used as the carriageway for other stately homes the BBC filmed at.

Above: **Loseley House, a key location for *Sense and Sensibility.***

These included Dorney Court in Windsor, Berkshire which served as the grand home of Sir John Middleton (played by Mark Williams). It is here that the lavish dinner party scene was filmed, as was the rehearsal for the ball the Dashwood sisters attend. Privately owned, it is a Grade I listed building of outstanding historical interest. "We have a lot of production companies interested in Dorney Court and several dramas have been filmed here," said Dorney Court's Robbie Gibbs. "The film of *The Other Boleyn Girl* was made in part in the house for example as was some of *Cranford*." See www.dorneycourt.co.uk for further details. The sumptuous 17th Century Ham House on the banks of the River Thames at Ham, Richmond-Upon-Thames doubled up as Cleveland. The house which belongs to the National Trust, has stunning formal gardens which have been partially restored, as well as gorgeous interiors and original collections. Go to www.national-trust.org.uk for information about visiting times. The spectacular Dyrham House, a William and Mary mansion set in a deer park, also belonging to the Trust was used to shoot many of the garden scenes. The location can also be glimpsed in the movie *Remains of the Day* shot in 1993. Finally, the splendid library at historic Loseley Park just outside Guildford, Surrey which is a stunning wedding venue for many a lucky bride, doubled up as Colonel Brandon's library. This impressive manor house just off the A3 has been used in a number of television dramas including *Midsomer Murders*, *Jane Eyre*, *Miss Marple* and *Spooks*. The front entrance of Loseley was also used in *Sense and Sensibility* for the scenes in which Colonel Brandon and his guests, including the Dashwoods gather in preparation for his picnic which doesn't happen as he is called away on urgent business. The House also doubled as the exterior of Sir John's home which of course was set in Devon in the story, while its impressive Oak Room was used in the series to nurse a sick Marianne after her walk in the rain. See www.loseley-park.com for more information.

Skins

Bristol

Teen drama *Skins* began airing on E4 then Channel 4 in 2007 and has proved to be a huge hit, particularly with youngsters who can identify with its modern-day issues such as relationship angst, infidelity, drugs and pressures of school. Focusing on a group of Bristol teenagers, the city itself is featured heavily throughout most episodes and a number of Bristol landmarks are readily recognisable such as Bristol Cathedral which is shown in the opening credits of series one and the Pur Down BT transmission tower situated to the right of the M32 as you enter Bristol, with wonderful views over the city in the opening credits of series two. The unit base for *Skins* is in a large warehouse in Fishponds, north Bristol. "They base themselves there then build sets there for house and club interiors," explained Natalie Moore of Bristol Film Office. "For exteriors they use Brandon Hill quite a lot." Brandon Hill is one of the city's oldest public parks, gifted to the council in 1147 by the Earl of Gloucester and boasting spectacular views across Bristol. Fans of *Skins* may recall the scene at the end of series one with Sid and Cassie sitting together on a park bench at dusk, gazing across the city. For details of opening times contact Bristol Parks on 0117 922 3719.

The last episode of series two involves a car chase which was filmed around Brandon Hill in Great George Street, while the set of stairs a car flies down was shot in Baldwin Street in Old Market. The majority of filming took place on Sundays when it was possible to close roads to traffic and pedestrians, all of which was organised through Natalie at Bristol Film Office with the help of Avon and Somerset Police and the Highways department of Bristol's City Council. Other parks and council- owned estates around Bristol used include The Kings Weston Estate, Oldbury Court Estate, Ashton Court Estate and Queens Square. Many college scenes were shot at John Cabot City Technology College, or John Cabot Academy as it is also known, in series one, an independent school in Kingswood, north east Bristol. "In series two, we decided to recreate a classroom and the headmaster's office on our set so as to use the real college a lot less," explained Location Manager Midge Ferguson, who has worked on ITV's *Primeval,* many episodes of *Casualty* and the drama *Afterlife* which was also filmed in Bristol. "We used the college mainly for exterior shots. When we did use John Cabot, we were mindful not to disrupt the real students and tended to shoot at weekends or after 4pm

"In the first series, some of the characters' homes were real houses but domestic locations can be a nightmare to film. It's just awkward filming in houses, filming in the same street over and over again, so once again, we built houses on our set and went and shot exteriors of characters going in and out of front doors, on location." About 200 yards from Brandon Hill is College Green which is at the bottom of Park Street, outside the council offices. It is here that the teens in *Skins* often congregate after class. "It's supposedly right outside their college when it's actually a completely different location," Midge said. "We built our own nightclub set but also used Lakota, La Rocca and The Croft which are well known clubs around the city." Other locations to look out for include Rocotillos, a 50s-style diner in Queen's Row where fans will recall Sid and Cassie kiss. The main Bristol University often doubled up for several different venues while the once-derelict Pro Cathedral was used as the venue for a huge 'secret party' in series two which was filmed exclusively for the Internet and to which 500 fans of the show were invited. After being dormant for 30 years, the building is now under major reconstruction.

To the Manor Born

Cricket St Thomas

The BBC had a winner on its hands in 1979 with its comedy series *To the Manor Born*. The show stars Penelope Keith as frightfully posh Audrey Fforbes-Hamilton who, stung by death duties, is forced to sell her stately home, Grantleigh Manor, and live in the estate's tiny lodge, taking her butler Brabinger and her beagle, Benjie, with her. Grantleigh Manor was bought by self-made millionaire grocer Richard De Vere who, certainly in the eyes of Mrs Fforbes-Hamilton, doesn't come from the right kind of background necessary to live in such a place. But he obviously grows on her, as they marry at the end of the series and were still together when the show returned for a special episode shown at Christmas 2007.

The series was filmed on the elegant Cricket St Thomas estate, near Chard in Somerset. Cricket House naturally played Grantleigh Manor and the estate's lodge played Mrs Fforbes-Hamilton's modest residence. *To the Manor Born* was written by Peter Spence, who lived near Cricket St Thomas and who is married to Jill, sister of the estate's former co-owner John Taylor. There were some real-life similarities between *To the Manor Born* and John's ownership of the estate. For example, both John and Richard De Vere bought their estates after the previous owner died and like Richard De Vere, John's mother lived at the house.

Above: (left) **Filming *To the Manor Born* at night** *(centre)* **Cricket St Thomas, alias Grantleigh Manor** *(right)* **the famous clapperboard.** *Opposite page:* **Penelope Keith and Peter Bowles filming the 2007 Christmas special.**

The estate was bought in 1998 by Warner Leisure Hotels and the house, which was built in 1785 and is Grade II listed, has been turned into a luxury resort hotel offering four-star accommodation. For details of how to book accommodation at Cricket St Thomas see www.warnerleisurehotels.co.uk Surrounding the house itself are 16 acres of beautiful gardens including a large Atlas Cedar tree, in the shade of which, it is said, once stood a seat on which Admiral Nelson and Lady Hamilton reputedly spent many an hour when the house was owned by Nelson's niece Charlotte.

The rest of the 100 acre estate is taken up by a wildlife park which conserves endangered species from around the world in a naturalistic environment and it also takes part in international breeding programmes. In addition to the animals, which include wallabies, a cheetah, leopards, waterbuck and lemurs there is forge and a scenic railway.

The Cricket St Thomas Wildlife Park is open to the public throughout the year. See www.wild.org.uk for details.

Having a wildlife park nearby made filming at the house a little unusual, as Peter Spence recalled: "Normally when you have to stop filming it's because of noise from aeroplanes or cars but at Cricket St Thomas 27 years ago it was because it was because of an elephant trumpeting or a sea lion squawking."

Wycliffe

Cornwall

In terms of stunning locations the ITV detective drama *Wycliffe* was the best television advertisement for the beautiful county of Cornwall, since *Poldark* was filmed by the BBC back in the 70s. Jack Shepherd (*pictured right*) stars as likeable Cornish sleuth Detective Superintendent Charles Wycliffe alongside his faithful team of Jimmy Yuill and Helen Masters as Detective Inspectors Doug Kersey and Lucy Lane.

Together they solve all manner of baffling cases during the show's five series which ran from a pilot episode in 1993 until 1998. The production base was Truro but locations all over Cornwall from quiet farmhouses and

pretty fishing villages to cliffs buffeted by raging seas and upmarket houses were used in the filming of the show.

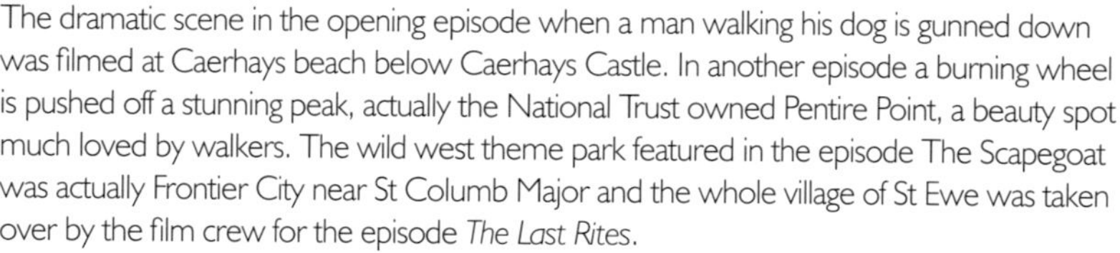

The dramatic scene in the opening episode when a man walking his dog is gunned down was filmed at Caerhays beach below Caerhays Castle. In another episode a burning wheel is pushed off a stunning peak, actually the National Trust owned Pentire Point, a beauty spot much loved by walkers. The wild west theme park featured in the episode The Scapegoat was actually Frontier City near St Columb Major and the whole village of St Ewe was taken over by the film crew for the episode *The Last Rites*.

Other key scenes were filmed at Porthleven, Redruth, Portreath, Goonhilly Down (the BT communications centre), Carharrach and Kennach Sands. The shot of an exploding fishing boat in the episode *The Pea Green Boat* was filmed off Godrevy Point near Hayle and a car going off a cliff in the same episode was filmed at Porthowan.

Also in the South West

Echo Beach

The ITV drama starring Martine McCutcheon and Jason Donavan is set in the fictional Cornish town of Polnarren. In actual fact it was filmed in Looe, Polperro and Watergate Bay (*pictured left*). Jason Donovan's character's surfboard shop and café was filmed at the Extreme Store, part of the www.watergatebay.co.uk hotel, where scenes were also filmed at its outside bar area. Some of the stars stayed there during filming.

Wild West

Filmed at Portloe, on the south Cornwall coast, which doubled as fictional St Gweep, Simon Nye's comedy stars Dawn French as lesbian Mary Trewednack, who runs the local shop with her partner Angela.

The South East

Bleak House

Hertford

Even audiences who had never thought Charles Dickens could be interesting could not help but be captivated by the BBC's adaptation of his classic *Bleak House* which was screened in the autumn of 2005. Penned by the talented Andrew Davies and produced by Nigel Stafford-Clark, their brief from the Head of Drama, Jane Tranter, was for it to be "Bold. Fresh. Imaginative." And it certainly was.

What makes *Bleak House* so eminently watchable is its large and impressive cast of household names. The American actress Gillian Anderson of *The X-Files* fame was the first to jump aboard as Lady Dedlock, much to the delight of casting director Kate Rhodes James, which left a mere 85 further roles to fill, 40 of them principal characters. After much discussion, sweat and tears, the job was done with such stars as Pauline Collins, Nathanial Parker, Alun Armstrong, Denis Lawson and Charles Dance to name but a few, all signed up and raring to go.

With such a massive cast and an ambitious number of hours to shoot, filming locations were more important than ever. Everyone involved realised it would be both time and cost-effective not to move around too much if possible and so it was decided that just one large house with the necessary historical features should be used to film various different locations as opposed to either building a set from scratch or indeed, moving from one venue to another.

Balls Park, a Grade I listed building just outside Hertford proved to be the ideal building for it had everything required to make it a practical first choice. "It even had a room we were able to use as Chancery which is at the heart of *Bleak House* and around which all the various stories revolve," explained Nigel Stafford-Clark.

Right: **Stunning Balls Park in Hertford was a great find by the *Bleak House* location manager and a key location for the series.**

Above: **Caddy Jellyby (Nathalie Press) embraces her mother Mrs Jellyby (Liza Tarbuck) in a scene from *Bleak House*.**

"The Balls Park mansion has this wood-panelled room which goes up three floors and up to the roof – no one could tell us what it had been used for – but it was just what we needed." So it was here that the likes of the interior of Bleak House itself, Tulkinghorn's offices and even the garrets above Krook's shop which were created in the eaves, came to life so convincingly. The interior of the big court room, Lincoln's Inn Court, was also filmed at Balls Park.

The exterior of Balls Park doubled up as the exterior of Boythorn's house and the 16th Century Ingatestone Hall in Essex served as the exterior of Bleak House. This stunning mansion set in formal gardens, is owned by the Petre family having first been acquired by Sir William Petre in 1539. It has been gradually modernised over the centuries and in 1989 when the 18th Lord inherited the property, he totally renovated it and opened it to the public. Tel 01277 353010 for details of opening times. Charles Dickens himself lived in Kent for many years and is known to have strolled through the grounds of the very impressive Cobham Hall, a 12th Century manor house set in 150 acres of Grade II listed parkland. The BBC used the exterior of the very same Cobham Hall as the exterior of Lady Dedlock's home, Chesney Wold. It also served as the exterior of the Inns of Court. The interior of the Hall was also used for some scenes. Go to www.cobhamhall.com to learn more about the Hall's history and for public opening times.

One of the concerns of Location Manager Nick Marshall was finding a suitable location to shoot Dickensian London exteriors but the logistics of them actually being in London would have proved time consuming and expensive. He struck lucky when he came across the perfect location, a discovery he considers one of his "professional highlights." Less than an hour from Balls Park, up the M1 motorway, the old farm yard of Luton Hoo was ingeniously transformed into the cobbled streets of London. This historic Grade I listed building is now a luxury five star hotel but half of the estate is still a working farm which proved perfect for the BBC's needs.

"We had an entirely controlled environment that didn't have problems with modern society taking place around it except for the aeroplane noise around Luton Hoo!" Nick said. "We were able to hire it for six months and do everything we needed to do, exactly how we wanted.

"The art department were able to build around and on top of the majority of the buildings and create our own down town London. We still had to go to a few other places such as Spitalfields in east London which still appears traditionally Georgian/Victorian, but many of our exterior requirements (as well as some interiors) were served by the Luton Hoo estate. A lot of the interior of the farm buildings were turned into the ground floor of Krook's and Snagsby's shops for instance, so we didn't have problems with continuity. And of course the existing cobbles among the farm buildings were ready to use as they were. I'd go back to film on the estate in a heartbeat if the right project came about. It has such an interesting history and is one of my favourite places."

The Darling Buds of May

Pluckley

The sleepy village of Pluckley in Kent had never expected the attention that it suddenly received in the summer of 1991. For the instant success of Yorkshire Television's The *Darling Buds of May,* starring the ever-popular David Jason as Pop Larkin, brought hordes of fans into the village, which is said to be one of the most haunted places in Britain. The quaint, 15th Century Black Horse pub played the Hare and Hounds in the series. "We still get people coming to the village because of *The Darling Buds of May*," said landlord Kevin Savidge. "And they also come here for the ghosts as we're one of the most haunted pubs in the country – and we've been on television quite a lot for that too."

Just across the road is the grocer's shop, which featured in the series, as did Pluckley Butchers shop next door. Nearby St Nicholas' Parish Church became a star attraction in the series when Mariette, played by Catherine Zeta Jones, married Charley (Philip Franks). It was also used when Primrose Larkin (Abigail Rokinson) was chasing the Reverend Candy, played by Tyler Butterworth.

Next door to the church is the house that played guide mistress Edith Pilchester's home and opposite the church is the small house, which played Orchard Cottage where the Brigadier, played by Moray Watson, lives. A few doors away is the local school which was used in the series as the village hall.

Above: (left) **David Jason as Pop Larkin** *(centre)* **The Black Horse pub, which doubled as The Hare and Hounds in the series** *(right)* **Pam Ferris, David Jason and Catherine Zeta Jones.**

A few miles away from Pluckley, on the road to Smarden, is Buss Farm, which played the Larkin's Home Farm. But the farm is private and not open to the public and it cannot be seen from the road. However, a classic car rally, in aid of two worthy charities takes place every year at the farm – see www.darlingbudsclassiccarshow.co.uk – so you could catch a glimpse of it and also see Pop Larkin's yellow Rolls Royce and the blue truck which was used for Mariette's wedding.

The Darling Buds of May production team stumbled on the farm after spending two weeks looking for the ideal location. "It was quite difficult to find something that fitted the bill," explained Production Designer Alan Davis. "The problem was that many of the houses had been renovated and dolled up."

The farmhouse still had to be repainted and a modern extension at the back of the house had to be disguised. "We decided to cover the whole thing in Kentish weatherboarding to make it look a bit more rural and in keeping with the local architecture," he said.

The next job was to add ivy and dead vine to the house. "We put ivy on to take the edge off the squareness of the place," said Alan. The dead vine went on first and then silk and plastic ivy - all bought by the sackload - was stapled on branch by branch.

The farmyard was Alan's biggest headache as it needed to be filled with 1950s junk. Alan and the show's prop buyer roamed the Kent countryside with a heavy lifting vehicle in convoy hunting for junk and snapped up everything that Pop Larkin would have littering his farmyard. "We got whatever we could find," said Alan. "We picked up tons of apple boxes, an old tractor, an old conveyer, apple picking ladders, barrels, general scrap metal, lots of oil drums, tyres, an old pitch boiling tank, an old water tank and any farm machinery we saw."

Above: **David Jason on location at Buss Farm, the main location for *The Darling Buds of May*.**

Alan was stumped by just one thing - nettles! Not too many of them, but too few. He explained: "In the book there are references to lots of nettles in amongst the scrap and junk but if there's one thing you can't transplant it is weeds!

"You can't actually dig up some nettles or thistles and put them in a pot and water them and expect them to grow because they never do. There's something about weeds that they just don't like being moved."

Some scenes in later episodes of the show, supposedly in Kent, were actually filmed hundreds of miles away in Yorkshire - to save time and money.

"It's a question of cost," explained David Jason. "The producers found that they could get locations in Leeds that looked like Kent. That way they could save money because they didn't have to ship the crew all the way down to Kent and pay for hotels there. As long as it looks like Kent and can convince us all then that's fine. They are very careful to make sure no one can say: 'That can never be Kent.'"

Fawlty Towers

Bourne End

Sadly the real house used on screen as the infamous *Fawlty Towers* hotel was bulldozed in early 1993. Wooburn Grange at Bourne End in Buckinghamshire, was ravaged by fire in March 1991 just before it was due to be renovated and was hit by a second blaze just four months later.

The building played an important role in the classic 70s BBC comedy which stars John Cleese as manic hotel boss Basil Fawlty, Prunella Scales as his domineering wife Sybil, Connie Booth as waitress Polly and Andrew Sachs as Manuel, the Spanish waiter.

Above: (top) **Basil Fawlty and his staff** *(bottom)* **Wooburn Grange, the setting for *Fawlty Towers*, was never actually in Torquay.**

Fawlty Towers hotel was supposed to be in Torquay in Devon but BBC bosses chose the Buckinghamshire site because it was nearer to London. After filming ended Wooburn Grange became a nightclub called Basil's and was later used as an Indian restaurant. By the spring of 1993 it had vanished completely and had been replaced by eight five bedroom family homes.

But *Fawlty Towers* fans can however visit other places associated with the series like Mentmore Close in north London where Basil beats his car with the branch of a tree in *Gourmet Night*. Just round the corner in Dovedale Avenue is St John's United Reformed Church which Basil is seen driving past in the same episode and the location for Andre's restaurant was 294 Preston Road in Harrow, which is now a Chinese restaurant called Wings.

The hospital used in *The Germans*, where Sybil has her in-growing toenail removed, was Northwick Park Hospital in Northwick Park. Or you could head off to Torquay where the Gleneagles Hotel, the inspiration for the show, is located. But don't expect Fawlty-style service, for as the hotel says on its website it has "been transformed from a place that inspired the BBC hit TV show *Fawlty Towers* into a modern boutique hotel typical of a place found in the world's most glamorous must visit cities and resorts."

It was a different case in 1971 when John Cleese and the rest of the Monty Python team stayed there. The behaviour of the then owner Donald Sinclair was lengendary. He who mistook Eric Idle's bag for a bomb, complained about the way Terry Gilliam used his knife and fork. The rest of the Pythons decamped to another hotel whereas John Cleese stayed on and was later joined by his then wife Connie Booth. The extra stay paid off as four years later *Fawlty Towers*, inspired by his Torquay trip, began.

In 2002 Cleese told the Torquay's *Herald Express*: "I do remember all the other Pythons left but Connie Booth and I were lazy. We stayed on and didn't realise we were accumulating material."

Foyle's War

Hastings

Foyle's War made its debut on ITV in 2002 and was considered an overnight hit. In fact it was the highest rated drama of that year, pulling in an amazing 10 million viewers and went on to win a BAFTA in 2003. Written and carefully researched by Anthony Horowitz, who also created the ever popular *Midsomer Murders*, the crime drama was set on the south coast of England during World War II. Series one began in 1940 while the final series six, was set at the end of the war in 1945. Detective Chief Superintendent Christopher Foyle, played by the convincing Michael Kitchen, investigates murders and other serious crime against a backdrop of 1940s England, touching on subjects such as internment and conscription dodging in the process.

The drama hit our screens at a time when other detective shows such as *Morse* had come to an end and seamlessly filled a void with its blend of brilliant writing, wonderful sets, costumes and actors. The attention to 1940s detail is one of the most impressive factors of *Foyle's War.* The production team went to great lengths to make every scene as authentic as possible and all evidence of modern day life such as television aerials, satellite dishes, modern streetlamps and burglar alarms had to be removed or disguised from areas used for filming. And of course road markings, street signs and today's cars had to be hidden too.

Below: **Michael Kitchen and Honeysuckle Weeks filming a *Foyle's War* scene in Hastings.**

Christopher Foyle lives in Hastings and it was here that a large chunk of all six series was shot. For instance, Steep Street is Foyle's house and a genuine home – the actual address used was in fact 31 Croft Road, a rather narrow street in the old town. The house is privately owned and let out to ITV for filming purposes.

The High Street, Post Office Passage and Church Street also regularly crop up in every series and like Croft Road, are narrow and restrictive and were usually closed off to the public while filming, not that residents raised objections. St Clements Church which can be found just off the High Street makes a regular appearance in *Foyle's War* as Sam (Honeysuckle Weeks) has to drive past it every time she visits Foyle at home. It was also used for a scene on a National Day of Prayer in one episode.

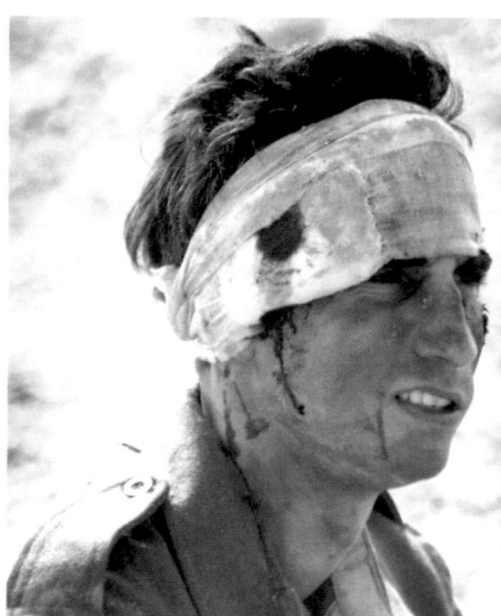

Above: (left) **A prop post box is carried into place** *(centre)* **a birds eye view of filming** *(right)* **Realism in *Foyle's War* included authentic looking war wounds.**

The pilot of *Foyles War* which was made in the summer of 2001, was shot in old town Hastings which proved to be an excellent choice of location. The beautiful beach with its close proximity to France and historic links to the war led Anthony Horowitz to make his lead character a Hastings resident and so a firm bond between Foyle and the town was forged. Locals are both delighted and proud to be connected to the series and there's even an official book on the subject, Foyle's Hastings which is a comprehensive guide to behind the scenes. To order a copy, go to www.1066country.com

Simon Allen, Film Liaison Officer for Hastings Borough Council, said the town grew to love *Foyle's War* over the years and like audiences worldwide, were saddened when the final episodes were filmed in 2007. "I worked on the pilot episode and every single series was shot here so as you can imagine, we formed good working relationships with the production team," he said.

"We at the council did everything we could to ensure that everything ran smoothly including closing off roads when necessary so by the time we got to series three and four, it was like a well-oil machine. We tended to roll out the same process every year because they (Greenlit Productions for ITV) generally wanted the same things.

"For example, they always wanted to film on the beach, their parking requirements were always the same and we always had to take down street signage to create a period effect. Hastings retains its name in the show as does Eastbourne and some local place names are also used but by and large, Anthony Horowitz fictionalises most names. I think Hastings is mentioned something like 30 times per episode! It's been very good for the town and I think it will long continue to have an effect with syndication and repeats.

"Hastings is a very popular location for filming anyway. A Michael Caine film (*Is There Anybody There?*) was shot here in 2007 and there are always requests from production companies under consideration."

Historic landmarks, the fishermen's net huts appeared in some episodes as did Hastings Pier which first opened in 1872. The Royal Victoria Hotel, St Leonards was the scene of a murder following a bombing raid. While filming took place, the A259 which runs outside the hotel, was temporarily closed – no small feat as it happens to be one of the busiest roads in the UK.

Other locations used to shoot *Foyle's War* include Squerryes Court in Westerham, Kent, a stunning 17th Century manor house surrounded by 20 acres of historic gardens. Telephone 01959 562345 or see www.squerryes.co.uk for information on opening times.

The market town of Midhurst, West Sussex was chosen to film an episode in series five and locals recall seeing the actors huddled under umbrellas in the March of 2006 as the rain poured down. Several locations in the town were employed, including Midhurst Bookshop in Knockhundred Row which became a hairdressers in the drama. The house adjoining the bookshop, Burgage House, was used as the Southern Bank.

Other places you might like to visit or to look out for when watching repeats of *Foyle's War* include Eastbourne Bandstand, the promenade area of which doubled up as a tea pavilion in two episodes; The Red Lion Pub in Fishpool Street, St Albans featured in an episode – as itself. It was actually called The Queen's Head in the script but the producers decided to rename it after seeing the pub's distinctive sign. And the privately-owned Tudor house, Stonewall Park in Chiddingstone, Kent, doubled up as Wing Commander Keller's office.

Above: (top) **Michael Kitchen and Honeysuckle Weeks filming in Hastings** *(bottom)* **Actors playing soldiers on Hastings beach.**

The Good Life

Northwood

The classic 70s comedy *The Good Life* sees Tom and Barbara Good turn their middle class home in Surbiton into a self-sufficient empire of vegetables and animals. At the time, it caused thousands to copy their idea and countless lawns all over the country were dug up and replaced by rows of carrots and turnips. Tom and Barbara's lifestyle, however, is far from ideal for their upmarket next-door neighbours Margo and Gerry Leadbetter, played by Penelope Keith and Paul Eddington, who awake each morning to the sound of pigs and hens. In the series Kewferry Road in Northwood, Middlesex doubled for the fictional road, The Avenue, Surbiton, Surrey, because it was easier for the crew and actors to travel from the BBC Television Centre to Northwood with their cameras and props than Surbiton. Finding two suitable houses side by side for the series, one slightly run-down and one immaculate could have been a problem but location managers struck lucky in Kewferry Road.

"They were very lucky," recalled Richard Briers. "Tom and Barbara's house was 1930s and a bit peeling and a little bit shabby and Gerry and Margo's was one of those Hendon type houses, very smart with bay windows and with a much smarter garden so we didn't have to do anything to it which was very lucky." Of course, the then owners of the Good's house, Number 55, had agreed to have both their fully-lawned front and back gardens dug up and covered with vegetables not to mention having animals running round - and one of their rooms doubling-up as a make-up and costume store. After each series a BBC crew dug up the vegetables and re-laid the turf - and after the final series the production team even added a patio for them. Playing host to *The Good Life* film crew wasn't always easy though. For one episode the Fire Brigade stood in the front garden spraying their hoses over the roof into the back garden as rain - turning the back garden into a site resembling the Somme.

Holby Blue

Surrey

Despite being a spin-off of hospital dramas *Casualty* and *Holby City*, cop series *Holby Blue* made by Kudos, is filmed nowhere near its sister shows. *Casualty* is shot in the Bristol area, *Holby City* at Elstree while relative newcomer *Holby Blue* which was first screened in 2007 is shot in Surrey. Starring a host of top names including Zoe Lucker, Kacey Ainsworth and James Thornton, *Holby Blue* is set in Holby Police Station which is actually filmed on a purpose-built set at a former Ministry of Defence complex near Chertsey. The massive, high-ceilinged space took months to be transformed into the police reception area, officers' locker room, holding cells, car park and offices. Corridors and a large steel staircase were built from scratch. The exterior of the station is shot at Brunel University in west London. Some of the cast spent time at nearby Woking Police Station shadowing uniformed officers and it was on Woking's cell block that the fictional version was designed. The towns of Chertsey, Woking and Egham are all used for exterior scenes such as car chases and gun battles with the location manager always on the look-out for buildings that resemble those in Bristol. Surrey of course is surrounded by hills and these always have to be careful avoided when cameras are being pointed.

Howard's Way

Bursledon

The BBC's 80s sex and sailing soap *Howard's Way* brought tourists flocking to south Hampshire where the series was filmed. It was set around the fictional village of Tarrant, played in real life by pretty Bursledon near Southampton. The series focusses on the Mermaid Boatyard owned by Tom Howard and Jack Rolfe and that was played by the Elephant Boatyard in Land's End Road. You can enjoy a quiet drink at the main pub used in *Howard's Way,* The Jolly Sailor just along the road. Halfway down Kew Road is Bondfield House, a private house which played the Howard family home in the series and just off Kew Lane is Hungerford where Hunt's Folly played the home of Jan's mother Kate Harvey. The other major location was St Leonard's Church in Church Lane, Hamble, which was used for the filming of Lynne Howard and Claude Dupont's wedding.

Above: **Howard's Way was usually filmed in Hampshire, but this picture of stars Tony Anholt, Jan Harvey, Ivor Danvers, Kate O'Mara and Stephen Yardley was taken on location in Malta.**

The BBC was very resourceful in its use of locations to save money, for example the Victoria Rampart Jetty at nearby Warsash doubled as New York harbour when Lynne Howard crosses the Atlantic single-handedly, the High Street at Hamble played Italy in one episode and Waddesdon Manor, a National Trust property near Aylesbury, Buckinghamshire played Charles Frere's French Chateau Auban. Exterior shots of Victoria Rampart offices were also used as Ken Master's chandlery and Jan Howard's boutique and scenes at Ken's powerboat centre were filmed at a real-life showroom on the A27 at Swanwick. The business park built by tycoon Charles Frere in the series is actually Arlington Securities' Solent Business Park, just off junction nine of the M27 and the marina that Frere builds is actually Hythe Marina, at Hythe, near Southampton.

It Ain't Half Hot Mum

Farnham

You could be mistaken for thinking that the BBC comedy *It Ain't Half Hot Mum,* which was set in wartime Burma, was actually filmed in a hot sticky climate. But that was just clever make-up. For the series, featuring the exploits of an army concert party, was actually filmed at BBC studios with the furthest location used being woods at Farnham in Surrey. And as with *Dad's Army*, the MoD allowed the BBC to film on its land, this time a wood. Clever set-dressing turned Farnham into Burma. Writer Jimmy Perry recalled: "We used to put rubber palms and rubber jungle creepers in the ground." The late Ken MacDonald, best-known as barman Mike Fisher in *Only Fools and Horses* was thrilled when he was given the part of banjo-playing Gunner Clark, particularly at the thought of filming in some exotic foreign location. "But we ended up in these woods in Farnham," he recalled in 1993. "But it was a great show to get into and tremendous fun." And although Michael Knowles, who plays dashing Captain Ashwood, loved working on the show, he doesn't miss the daily routine he faced on the set of *It Ain't Half Hot Mum* - being covered in fake sweat. "It was agony," he said. "We had a lot of lighting to make it look hot and they used to spray this glycerine and water stuff on us and the sand would blow up and stick on you."

Jonathan Creek

Shipley

Jonathan Creek isn't your average television detective and it's therefore quite apt that he doesn't have a typical home. In fact Jonathan's home couldn't really have been more unusual. After all, how many other television characters live in a windmill? In David Renwick's cleverly crafted mystery series, the eponymous hero, played by Alan Davies and his investigative crime writer colleagues Maddy Magellan, played by Caroline Quentin, and later Carla Borrego (Julia Sawalha) solves seemingly impossible crimes.

Originally the production team making *Jonathan Creek* hoped to find a windmill near to their base at Teddington Studios but that didn't work out as Production Designer John Asbridge explained: "Our location manger had been driving round the countryside but it soon became apparent that we were going to go away from London for the mill because we just couldn't find what we needed that close to London because by their very nature these places tend to be out in the countryside.

"Even after we starting looking a bit further afield it took some time to find the right mill. Some were cheek-by-jowl with a modern bungalow or house, others had been desperately converted and were just miserable with awful double-glazing. The other problem was if people were living in the mill we knew we'd have to have them out and we'd then have to totally redecorate and furnish what essentially was their home.

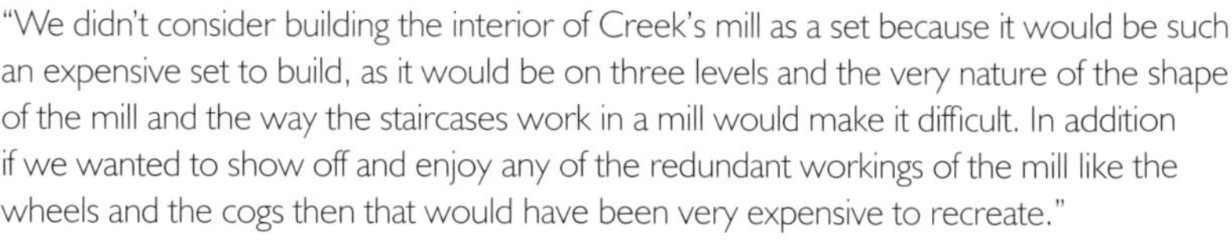

"We didn't consider building the interior of Creek's mill as a set because it would be such an expensive set to build, as it would be on three levels and the very nature of the shape of the mill and the way the staircases work in a mill would make it difficult. In addition if we wanted to show off and enjoy any of the redundant workings of the mill like the wheels and the cogs then that would have been very expensive to recreate."

Below: ***Jonathan Creek*** **star Alan Davies on location at Shipley Windmill.**

Eventually the location manager discovered Shipley Mill in west Sussex, a former home of the writer Hilaire Belloc, which is now owned by a Trust and therefore not lived in. Tucked away down a quiet lane and overlooking a meadow, it was just what the production team needed.

Despite its looks, it's actually the youngest – and the largest – windmill in Sussex having been built in 1879 for a Mr Frend Marten by Horsham millwrights Grist and Steele and cost £2,500. In 1906 the mill, nearby Kings Land house and the surrounding land was bought by Hilaire Belloc. With the advent of freely available electricity and motor vehicles, windmills across Britain began to be used less often as they became uneconomic to run. Shipley Mill however combated this for a while by having a steam engine fitted that enabled it to be used on days when there was no wind and the mill continued to be used until the end of its active life in 1926.

Finally big roller mills put windmills like Shipley out of business. Between the wars Hilaire Belloc tried to keep the windmill in good order but the shortage of materials during the Second World War meant that by the time of Belloc's death in 1953 it needed considerable work to halt its decline.

An appeal was launched to restore the mill as a memorial to Hilaire Belloc and a local committee was formed which gained the support of the West Sussex County Council and it was reopened in 1958. In 1986 major repairs were again needed and a charitable Trust was formed consisting of various council representatives, the Friends of Shipley Windmill, the Society for the Protection of Ancient Buildings, the Book Trust and Charles Eustace, Belloc's great grandson who has given the Trust a 20- year lease at a peppercorn rent.

In 1990, thanks to grants and donations, the mill was re-opened, with just a single pair of sails, but a year later further donations meant a second pair could be added, restoring the mill to its former glory.

Shipley Windmill is open to the public – see www.shipleywindmill.org.uk for details – but you won't find any permanent reminders of *Jonathan Creek* other than photographs, because all Jonathan's artefacts used for filming were brought along by the BBC's design team and then returned to prop hire companies afterwards.

Jonathan Creek is actually a small town by Kentucky Lake, Kentucky, in the United States, which writer David Renwick and his wife Ellie had visited when he was planning the series. 'We were driving west from North Carolina, heading for Mississippi and the deep south, and suddenly here was this picturesque little inlet," he recalled. "It was all very serene and idyllic, and we got a room at this old, timbered motel surrounded by pine forests.

"Who can say why the name clicked? But something about it - the rhythm, maybe a slightly Dickensian feel it had - led me to file it away in my head for later. It meant that when I finally came to write the show the one thing I was certain about was the guy's name, and therefore the title of the show."

Above: **Stunning Shipley Windmill, the location for *Jonathan Creek*.**

Lady Chatterley

The Isle of Wight

The Isle of Wight doubled for the South of France for the controversial 1993 BBC production of *Lady Chatterley* which stars Joely Richardson in the title role and Sean Bean as her gardener Mellors. The Old Park Hotel at St Lawrence (01983 852583) was the location for the beach and woodland walk scenes and the clifftop theme park, Blackgang Chine and Lisle Combe, the house at the Rare Breeds and Waterfowl Park at St Lawrence, played Lady Chatterley's father's south of France home, Mandalay.

Havenstreet Station, part of the Isle of Wight Steam Railway, which runs from Wootton to Smallbrook Junction was featured in the final episode of the BBC adaptation when Lady Chatterley returns home from France.

The final scene where Mellors and Connie embrace at the stern of a ship as they set off for Canada, was filmed on the Southampton to Isle of Wight Red Funnel ferry "Cowes Castle" which is now no longer in service with the company. The ship doubled as a cross-channel cruise liner sailing from Southampton water. It was picked because it had a traditional wooden handrail and by cleverly filming from different angles Director Ken Russell was able to make the ferry look like a liner.

Men Behaving Badly

Worthing

The town of Worthing in West Sussex featured heavily in the second episode of the final trilogy of the hilarious BBC comedy *Men Behaving Badly,* broadcast over three nights during Christmas 1998. The story sees Gary, played by Martin Clunes, (*pictured left with the rest of the cast*) having to attend a security equipment conference in the town and his girlfriend Dorothy (Caroline Quentin), pal Tony (Neil Morrissey) and his girlfriend Deborah (Leslie Ash) decide to come along too.

They stay at the aptly named Groyne View Hotel in Worthing, which isn't the most romantic venue for a seaside break, especially when all four of them are sharing one room with peeling wallpaper. And while Tony, Dorothy and Deborah entertain themselves during the day with crazy golf, Gary becomes preoccupied with an attractive female delegate at the conference. Tony and Deborah step in to save Gary and Dorothy's relationship, and the crazy golf course comes off worst.

In real life the building used as the Groyne View Hotel isn't a hotel at all and is actually Crown Agents International Management Training Centre, 3-10, Marine Parade. The company, which specialises in training overseas civil servants, let the BBC use the outside of the building and the lounge and bar area for the conference scene. It was a perfect setting as the building used to be a three-star hotel.

The pier was used, as was the beach just to the east of the pier where Tony and Gary get drunk in a mock-up car. Flash Point, at the end of the promenade, was also used for the crazy golf course where Gary and Tony have a fight.

Midsomer Murders

Chilterns

While the fictional county of Midsomer might be one of the prettiest places in England – it is also clearly one of the most unfortunate as dark deeds and murder are highly frequent occurrences. In fact it has a murder rate which is probably one of the worst in the world. But fortunately, in the long-running crime drama series *Midsomer Murders*, there is a detective in the shape of dependable Detective Chief Inspector Tom Barnaby, played by John Nettles, who has no shortage of murders to solve among a population of wealthy and eccentric characters.

Barnaby, who is married to Joyce, (Jane Wymark), with a daughter Cully, played by Laura Howard, has had three sidekicks over the years - DS Gavin Troy (Daniel Casey), DS Dan Scott (John Hopkins) and currently DS Ben Jones (Jason Hughes). Since airing, the series has attracted a stellar guest cast including George Baker, Simon Callow, Ruth Gemmell, Emily Mortimer, Richard Briers, Kevin McNally, Orlando Bloom, Timothy West, Celia Imrie, Samantha Bond and George Cole.

Midsomer Murders, is actually filmed in locations all across the south east of England including Oxfordshire, Buckinghamshire, Surrey, Berkshire and Hertfordshire. Pick a picturesque village in one of these counties and it's quite likely that it has appeared in the series, which began in 1997, at some point. *Midsomer* camera crews and cast have also been spotted along the beach front in Brighton, Sussex and in Devon.

Not surprisingly with so many murders, there have been a fair few funerals in the high mortality drama and an array of different churches used to send off the departed as well as for weddings and village gatherings. Among those featured are Beaconsfield

Right: **Jason Hughes as DS Ben Jones and John Nettles as DCI Tom Barnaby on location at Loseley Park.**

Church, Buckinghamshire which has been used as two different churches in different episodes including *Death's Shadow* where Barnaby and Troy go to arrest the vicar; the interiors of Bray Church in Berkshire for a bell ringing scene; the 14th Century church in Brightwell Baldwin, Oxfordshire is spotted in a few different episodes; the church at Brill, Buckinghamshire which also features in *Four Funerals and a Wedding* and St Mary's Church in Haddenham, Buckinghamshire, which can be seen in *Judgement Day*, *A Talent for Life, Birds of Prey*, *Orchid Fatalis* and *Vixen's Run*. Bledlow Church in the same county, doubled up as Badger's Drift Church in *The Killings at Badgers Drift*.

Many picturesque pubs feature in *Midsomer Murders*, including The Cock & Rabbit in The Lee in Buckinghamshire where Barnaby enjoys more than a pint or two; The Crown in Cuddington which has cropped up in *Death in Disguise*, *Death of a Stranger*, *Death and Dreams* and *Bad Tidings*; the oldest freehouse in England, The Royal Standard of England, Forty Green, appeared in *Death in Chorus*; The Plough in Great Haseley, Oxfordshire; the renowned George and Dragon in Quainton, Buckinghamshire and in the same county, The Bell in Chearsley, which doubled as The Woodman in one episode. The pretty pub The Lions at Bledlow has appeared on eight occasions and doubles as The Queens Arms.

The village of Turville, Buckinghamshire, crops up in several Midsomer episodes - *Murder on St Malley's Day*, *Who Killed Cock Robin* and *The Straw Woman* - and the local pub, the Bull and Butcher even sells Midsomer Burgers. Equally at home on the cover of a chocolate box and in the same county is Long Crendon which can be seen in *Garden of Death, Tainted Fruit*, *Death & Dreams*, *Things that go bump... Dead Letters, A Tale of Two Hamlets* and *Second Sight*. The 15th Century courthouse at the end of the High Street featured in *Dead Letters.*

Waddesdon Manor which is situated between Aylesbury and Bicester in Buckinghamshire, a French-style chateau built by the banker, Baron Ferdinand de Rothschild can be spotted in *Death of a Stranger*. With its splendid gardens, it is perfect for weddings, corporate events or just to visit. Go to www.waddesdon.org.uk for further information. The secluded and pretty village of Bledlow also pops up in *Midsomer* episodes, *Dead Man's Eleven*, *Blue Herrings*, *Dark Autumn* and *The Maid in Splendour* and also in at least one episode of ITV's *Miss Marple*.

The village of Haddenham was used in the episodes *Judgement Day*, *A Talent for Life*, *Birds of Prey, Orchid Fatalis* and *Vixens Run* while Little Marlow featured in *Faithful unto Death, Tainted Fruit* and *Sauce for the Goose*. Joyce Barnaby joined other judges at Marlow's Danesfield Hotel www.danesfieldhouse.co.uk to choose the perfect village in *Judgement Day.* Old Amersham was seen in *Death of a Hollow Man*, *Death in Disguise, Blue Herring, Who Killed Cock Robin* and *Sauce for the Goose* and The Crown Hotel appeared in the Hugh Grant film *Four Weddings and Funeral.* The village of Hambleden featured in *Blood Will Out*, *Down Among the Dead Men* and *Who Killed Cock Robin*. The village also appeared in *Chitty Chitty Bang Bang, 101 Dalmatians, Sleepy Hollow, Band of Brothers, A Village Affair, Poirot*, *Rosemary & Thyme* and *Down to Earth*.

Great Missenden appeared in *Painted in Blood* and the bank used for filming is now a museum in honour of writer Roald Dahl who lived in the village. See www.roalddahlmuseum.org for details. The Lee was used in the first episode *The Killings at Badger's Drift*, and in *Death's Shadow*, *Death of a Stranger* and *Painted in Blood*.

Below: **Elizabeth Thomas (Rachel Smith) and John Nettles in a scene from the episode *Blood Will Out*.**

Dorney Court, Berkshire has also appeared along with Buckinghamshire Railway Centre at Quainton, which was seen in *Things that Go Bump in the Night* and *Down Among the Dead Men* and Holloway College, Egham, Surrey, the Henley Regatta, Henley, the Tiptree Jam Factory in Essex and Chalgrove Manor, Oxfordshire have also all featured.

Wallingford, which doubles as the fictional town of Causton, where Barnaby is based, has been used many times including *Midsomer Rhapsody, Orchid Fatalis* and *Tale of Two Hamlets*, and in 2008 a *Midsomer Murders* convention was held there at The Corn Exchange used in a numbers of episodes including *Stranglers Wood* and *Death's Shadow* as the fictional Causton Playhouse. Loseley Park near Guildford, Surrey, which is open to the public, was heavily featured in *They Seek Him Here* where it doubled up as Magna Manor, a shooting location for a film of *The Scarlet Pimpernel*. For further details telephone the Estate Office on 01483 304440 or go to www.loseley-park.com

The church of St Peter and St Paul in Dinton, Buckinghamshire, which dates back to the 15th Century, was used for a wedding scene in *Who Killed Cock Robin*, while in nearby Westlington Green, a body is found in a well in *Dead Letters*. On a happy note, at least for Barnaby who can't have much good news in his line of work, his daughter Cully finally married Simon Dixon, played by Sam Hazeldine, in an episode entitled somewhat chillingly as *Blood Wedding*. The wedding scenes were filmed at St Mary's Parish Church in Denham.

Mrs Brown

Isle of Wight

Much of the shooting of the BBC film *Mrs Brown*, which tells the poignant and unusual love story between Queen Victoria, played by Dame Judi Dench, and her loyal Highland ghillie John Brown, played by Billy Connolly, took place at Queen Victoria and Prince Albert's real-life retreat, Osborne House on the Isle of Wight.

Victoria married Albert in 1840 three years after she had come to the throne and they bought the site in 1845 and replaced the existing house with Thomas Cubitt's design for a new home, the building that we see now. It was completed in 1851 and is now in the care of English Heritage. See www.english-heritage.org.uk for details.

Above: **Osborne House, one of the main settings in *Mrs Brown*.**

The Royal couple found tranquillity at Osborne House with its fine views across the Solent and elegant Italian style away from the formality of court life at Buckingham Palace and Windsor Castle. Victoria said of it: "It is impossible to imagine a prettier spot."

Queen Victoria died on 22nd January 1901 on a couch bed in the Queen's Bedroom. The private royal suite was closed to all except members of the royal family until Queen Elizabeth II gave permission for full public access in 1954.

Of course much of *Mrs Brown* was filmed in Scotland. Privately owned 14th Century Duns Castle, on the Scottish borders near the market town of Duns, had a prominent role and if you fancy living like royalty, the castle offers accommodation and is available for weddings. See www.dunscastle.co.uk for more details.

Queen Victoria's waterfall picnic was filmed at a waterfall on the River Pattack near Loch Laggan. Other scenes were shot at Wilton House, Wilton, Wiltshire, which has also been used for the films *Sense & Sensibility*, *The Madness of King George* and *Pride & Prejudice*. See www.wiltonhouse.co.uk for details.

Osterley Park House, Isleworth, Middlesex, which also appeared in Cranford, was also used as was Luton Hoo, in Bedfordshire, a veteran of more than 20 films and TV shows including the Bond film *The World Is Not Enough*, *Four Weddings and a Funeral* and *Bleak House*.

The Office

Slough

The Office certainly put Slough on the map with millions of television viewers – but perhaps not in a way that the Berkshire town's local council might have liked, as it doesn't exactly suggest it is a happening place. Of course Ricky Gervais and Stephen Merchant's brilliant workplace spoof fly-on-the-wall comedy was mainly filmed at Teddington Studios but the show's iconic opening title sequence was shot in Slough.

The Brunel bus station and car park appear, as does the nearby Brunel Roundabout. The building on the Slough Trading Estate used for the exterior for the Wernham Hogg office in the opening titles was Crossbow House, Liverpool Road, Slough, although there is talk of the area being redeveloped in the future which could see Crossbow House disappearing which would be a shame as it is one of the most recognisable buildings on television.

Right: **Crossbow House in Slough, used as the exterior for *The Office*.**

Porridge

St Albans

Ball and chain jokes often feature at weddings at St Albans Register Office in Victoria Street, but that's perhaps predictable as it is housed in the former gatehouse to St Albans Prison. But the register office has an even greater claim to fame - it was the setting for the classic television comedy *Porridge* where Norman Stanley Fletcher does his lengthy stretch.

The real Victorian St Albans Prison, which had room for 85 men and 14 women, saw four executions, the last one being in 1914, but it hadn't been used as a real prison for decades when the BBC borrowed it as the front of HM Prison Slade. Designers put up the Slade signs, barred nearby windows and built a set of double doors at the end of the gatehouse entrance tunnel. The gatehouse was

Right: **The exterior for Slade Prison in St Albans - now a register office.**

used after the Home Office refused to allow the BBC to film at an actual prison. Exterior scenes set within the walls of Slade Prison were filmed at various psychiatric hospitals around London.

It became St Albans Register Office in 2004 after being home to St Albans Highways Department for many years and offices have now been built behind the gatehouse. "We trade on the *Porridge* connection and it is known locally as the old *Porridge* building," said Deputy Superintendent Registrar Claire Cook. "We still have the old prison doors which are attractive for photographs when they are closed. People – usually grooms – constantly make jokes about it being appropriate to get married at an old prison!"
The Home Office has relaxed its bar on filming in prisons since *Porridge* began in 1974 and now allows television companies to film in prisons for a fee, although much of the ITV drama hit *Bad Girls* was filmed at former Oxford Prison, which has now been converted into a hotel. See www.oxfordprison.co.uk for details.

The Vicar of Dibley

Turville

The BBC comedy series *The Vicar of Dibley* became a huge hit for the BBC and creator Richard Curtis. It stars Dawn French as Dibley vicar Reverend Geraldine Granger, whose pastoral work isn't always easy in a village full of quicky characters like Hugo (James Fleet), Alice (Emma Chambers), Owen (Roger Lloyd Pack) and Jim (Trevor Peacock).

Exterior scenes for the series were filmed in the Buckinghamshire village of Turville with the local church St Mary The Virgin, which dates back to the 12th Century, doubling as fictional St Barnabus Church. The exterior for the screen vicarage is actually two cottages in the

Right: **The beautiful village of Turville which plays Dibley.**

village which are made to look like one house, but interior shots were filmed weeks later at the BBC studios in London, with a fake backdrop in place at the front door for continuity.

Turville is no stranger to film crews as a nearby windmill, which overlooks the village, was used for the classic 1968 film *Chitty Chitty Bang Bang,* which stars Dick Van Dyke and Sally Ann Howes, and for the 1996 live action version of *101 Dalmatians*.

It was also used as the village of Weirfold for the ITV wartime drama *Goodnight Mister Tom* which stars John Thaw as widowed and cantankerous Tom Oakley whose life is changed when nine-year-old Willie Beech is billeted with him. More recently Turville has been used for episodes of *Midsomer Murders.*

Left (top). **St Mary The Virgin Church in Turville, which plays St Barnabus in *The Vicar of Dibley*** *(bottom)* **Another view of the pretty village of Turville**

Also in The South East

The Brittas Empire
The BBC comedy about the exploits of Whitbury Leisure Centre manager Gordon Brittas, played by Chris Barrie, was filmed at Ringwood Recreation Centre at Ringwood in Hampshire. The centre continued to be open to the public even when the series was being filmed. "We'd book the sports hall for a day just like anyone else would," recalled producer Mike Stephens. "And the same with the pool and the rest of it."

The location was picked for two reasons, as Mike explained: "Basically I wanted somewhere that looked different and it has certainly got a different style to it and also Chris was appearing in a play at Winchester while we were filming so we needed to find somewhere that he could get to easily each day."

Above: **Alex Ferns starred as a Royal Navy captain in *Making Waves*.**

Making Waves
ITV had high hopes for its Royal Navy drama *Making Waves* - and so they should have. After all the Ministry of Defence had loaned producers a huge prop - Type 23 frigate HMS Grafton to play fictional HMS Suffolk and the show had a solid cast including former *EastEnders* star Alex Ferns (pictured left) as Suffolk's CO and *Coronation Street* favourite Lee Boardman as a wise-cracking chef. But the series bombed and unusually was taken off air before all of its six episodes had been screened.

The cast and crew had spent many months filming the multi-million pound show in Portsmouth including at the Dockyard and at other locations all over the city including at the popular Gunwharf Quays shopping and restaurant waterfront development. For details see www.gunwharf-quays.com

Ruth Rendell Inspector Wexford Mysteries
Most major towns in Hampshire were used at some point for the filming of the *Ruth Rendell Inspector Wexford Mysteries* which began in 1988 and ran until 2000. The country detective, played by veteran actor George Baker, was based at Kingsmarkham played by the town of Romsey near Southampton. The side entrance of the town's Magistrates Court doubled as the entrance to the police station with the production team adding just a sign and putting police cars in the car park to make it look like the real thing.

Many streets in the centre of Romsey were featured in the stories and most restaurants and cafes were used at some point along with the Job Centre, Romsey Abbey, the Corn Market and Palmerston Square. Two pubs, the Queen Vic and the King William IVth played Wexford's locals and the house that played his home is also in the town. Outside Romsey, St John's Church at Farleigh Chamberlayne near Braishfield was used for a funeral scene, an Indian restaurant called Kuti's in London Road, Southampton, was used for one episode, Sherfield Parish Hall doubled as a police control centre and Southampton University was used as Brighton University.

Interior scenes for the story Speaker of Mandarin, which were supposed to be at a hotel in China, were actually shot at the Botley Park Hotel in Botley. The Kings Theatre in Southsea played a cinema and The Fuzz and Furkin pub, a former real police station, in Albert Road, Southsea, played a police station.

London

Ashes to Ashes

For the millions who adored *Life on Mars*, the follow up *Ashes to Ashes* was eagerly awaited and sparked an on-going debate as to whether the latter is as good as the former. Whatever one's opinion, this series pays just as much attention to period detail in its locations, being set in 1980s London, as opposed to 1970s Manchester. Incidentally, the first series attracted more than six million viewers.

Whereas *Life on Mars* features Sam Tyler, a modern detective who finds himself back in 1973 after a car crash, *Ashes to Ashes* works on the same premise except this time, DI Alex Drake, a bright, feisty psychological profiler played by Keeley Hawes, is propelled from 2008 back to 1981. Here she teams up with the ever-macho Detective Chief Inspector Gene Hunt (Philip Glenister) and theirs proves an often tempestuous pairing.

Three main locations which feature regularly throughout the series – CID, Alex's flat and Luigis restaurant - are all sets built at Kudos's production space in Bermondsey, south east London.

"It's in the same space as *Spooks* actually," revealed Mark Grimwade, who was Location Manager for some of *Ashes to Ashes* series one. "They would move out, we would move in and when we had moved out, *Hustle* would move in so they have (production company Kudos) got a permanent build space where they take one set down and put up another."

The exterior of the police station in *Ashes to Ashes* was actually shot at an empty building owned by the Stock Exchange on Christopher Street, EC2, London, by Finsbury Square. And conveniently, on the same street is a restaurant called Alexander's which doubled up as Luigis.

"With any exteriors you have to find buildings that are pre-1980s which can be anything from 100 years old up to 1981 so it can be quite difficult to find. A lot of *Ashes to Ashes* was based around the river and the docks and to find those sorts of places which haven't been developed is pretty tricky," said Mark.

"It was also meant to be based all around the Docklands area in east London and of course a lot of that has been developed. You just find certain streets which have parts that are still old fashioned and you have to be clever with the camera as to what you point at and what you don't."

Fans of the show will recall scenes on the River Thames which were shot near London's Royal Docks when Hunt and the boys race to Alex's rescue on a speed boat at the end of the first episode. Old, disused mills doubled up as wharf-side buildings with Tower Bridge as the backdrop.

Other locations used include a club next door to Caesar's (London's oldest nightclub) in Streatham Hill. It was here that a gay club scene was shot. In another episode, the real

Steve Strange, a club scene fixture in the 80s, was invited to the Blitz Club. This was in fact a snooker hall dressed to recreate the famous club and real Blitz Club fans appear as very enthusiastic extras with 80s perms, shoulder pads or 'new romantic' costumes.

Mark said part of the struggle with shooting period drama in the streets is clearing it of modern day cars which have to be replaced with period cars. Residents in selected areas such as Lewisham, large sections of which haven't been gentrified, received letters asking them to move their vehicles.

"Most of the time they were very co-operative and didn't mind helping us," he said "When a parked car couldn't be moved for any reason, we had to park a period car in front of it.

"We shot a lot in Southwark and they're brilliant. Some councils are less keen on the idea of filming but luckily, Southwark are happy about it and without their help, making *Ashes to Ashes* just wouldn't have been possible."

Below: **Philip Glenister as DCI Gene Hunt, Keeley Hawes as DI Alex Drake and the famous Audi Quattro in a scene from *Ashes to Ashes*.**

The Bill

Television's best known police station Sun Hill has actually been at three locations in the capital. When *The Bill* began in 1984 the production base was a single-storey office and warehouse complex in Artichoke Hill, Wapping in east London. By 1986 the production had outgrown the Wapping site and plans to make the series twice weekly had necessitated a move to bigger premises. In 1986 a redbrick, former record company distribution warehouse in Barlby Road, north Kensington became Sun Hill number two. The Victorian building, with an arched doorway, was well suited to its role and became a popular home for the series among both actors and production team. When Thames TV's lease on the building ran out in 1989 the owners announced that they were going to turn the site into a shopping centre and *The Bill* had to look for a new home .

Right: **The current exterior of Sun Hill police station in *The Bill*.**

Finding a new base for the set - and all the production suites - proved far from easy, but eventually Thames decided upon a former wine warehouse in Deer Park Road, Merton, but you cannot visit the set and would have to be lucky to catch anything actually being filmed as most scenes are shot inside the studio or away at other locations anywhere in south and south west London.

Producing two episodes of the series was never easy at the best of times, but trying to move a whole set and carry on filming at the same time was a mammoth logistical task. Extra episodes were stockpiled but there was another consideration - how to 'move' Sun Hill on screen without leaving viewers wondering why the now familiar Sun Hill police station suddenly looked different. This was done by writing a modernisation of the fictional station into the storyline. This allowed for portable cabins, scaffolding and junk to be strewn around the exterior of the station to cover the move. And the writers had another trick up their sleeves - they wrote an episode in which a huge car bomb blew up part of the station killing popular PC Ken Melvin (played by Mark Powley). The new studio was bigger than the two previous ones which has meant the series has been able to grow as the programme has developed and over the years extra sets have been added like a courtroom and a hospital set for the fictional St Hugh's Hospital. *The Bill* is unusual among television productions in that all the studios are real buildings. Most television sets are three-sided allowing room for a camera team. *The Bill's* offices and cells are all real solid areas which look just like the real thing both on screen and off.

EastEnders

Borehamwood

EastEnders is a problem for location fans because there is very little for them to actually see as the show is shot almost entirely on a specially built set at Elstree Studios in Borehamwood, Hertfordshire.

The Albert Square set we see on screen was based on real-life Fassett Square in Hackney - which obviously can be visited - and although the buildings look real on screen they are actually constructed from fibreglass and plasterboard, although some of it is real brick as some later sections, such as George Street, are faced with real brick.

The construction of the set took place between May and November 1984. The show's original design team wanted Albert Square to look old and established and as authentic as possible.

At the same time, they were concerned that the 'fake' buildings would not to be able to withstand the ravages of the British climate and didn't hold out much hope of them lasting more than three years. Little did they know, more than two decades later, the original Albert Square would still be standing.

Below: **It all looks so real - but Albert Square is a specially built set at a studio at Borehamwood, Hertfordshire.**

Said the late designer Keith Harris: "After the hurricane of October 1987 I came to check the set with a feeling of impending doom. The roads were blocked with the fallen trees and when I got to Elstree the security guards told me the damage was pretty bad. Expecting the worst, I approached the set to discover that luckily it was virtually untouched by the violent storms - the security guards had been having me on."

The Albert Square houses actually have no backs as the interior shots are filmed at an adjacent studio. When the set was first built it had just three sides and Bridge Street but over the years various buildings have been added including the bookies, Beale's Plaice, George Street and Walford East Tube Station.

EastEnders is a working set, so the BBC can't accommodate visitors, but *EastEnders* fans can visit various locations used on the programme which aren't inside Elstree Studios. For example, Den Watts was shot by the side of the Grand Union Canal, near Water Road, London NW10, Lofty and Michelle's marriage was filmed at the chapel in the grounds of Shenley Hospital, Shenley in Hertfordshire and Charlie Cotton's funeral, which coincided with the blessing of Ricky and Sam's marriage, was filmed at St Nicholas' Church, Elstree Hill, but most church scenes set in Walford are filmed at St Andrew's Church, Watford.

Pauline Fowler's and Frank Butcher's funerals were filmed at Hendon Crematorium in north London, Windsor Racecourse was used for scenes featuring Alfie and Kat, and Den's funeral took place at North Watford Cemetery, where a fake gravestone was put in place showing that Den was buried in the same grave as Angie. Walford's Register Office is usually Watford or Hendon Town Hall and if a court scene is required the location is in St Albans or Hatfield.

Above: **Rita Simons (Roxy Mitchell) and Samantha Janus (Ronnie Mitchell) filming *EastEnders* on location in Weymouth, Dorset in 2008.**

Over the years some episodes of *EastEnders* have been filmed abroad, in Amsterdam, Paris, Venice, Ireland, Normandy in France, Portugal and Marbella and Torremolinos in Spain and many scenes have been filmed in different parts of the UK including Blackpool, Manchester, Brighton, Portsmouth, Nottingham and Weymouth .

By the spring of 2008 there was talk that a new identical Albert Square might be built 28 miles away at Pinewood Studios as the current set was not suitable for High Definition (HD) filming as it would show too scenery defects like cracks, chips and patching.

Goodnight Sweetheart

The BBC comedy series *Goodnight Sweetheart* stars Nicholas Lyndhurst as Gary Sparrow, the man who juggles two women in different time zones, one modern day and the other during the Second World War. Unlike *Doctor Who*, we never see how Gary manages to travel in time, he simply walks down a passageway off a London street and switches time. The passageway, Ducketts Passage, where he walks is actually Ezra Street near the flower market off Columbia Road, Bethnal Green.

His 1940s wife Phoebe, played by Liz Carling, runs a pub The Royal Oak, and its exterior was played by the real-life Royal Oak at 73 Columbia Road. The pub has also been featured in the film *Lock, Stock and Two Smoking Barrels*, the BBC series *The Hello Girls* and *Eastenders* star Barbara Windsor popped in during her appearance in the BBC genealogy show *Who Do You Think You Are?* as her grandfather used to drink there. The modern day exterior of Gary's wartime memorabilia shop Blitz and Pieces was in nearby Old Street and the interior was a studio set. For more details go to: www.royaloaklondon.com

Right: **The Royal Oak which played the wartime pub in *Goodnight Sweetheart*.**

London's Burning

Real life Dockhead Fire Station was used as the fictional Blackwall Station in the long-runnning ITV drama series *London's Burning* and played home to the Blue Watch crew. For the original 1986 90-minute *London's Burning* film, from which the series began, the whole of the Dockhead was used for filming. Makers London Weekend Television had full cooperation from the London Fire Brigade and the production team put portable cabins in the station yard for the real fire-fighters to use for the six-week duration of filming. The cabins were used to replace the fire-fighters' relaxation area, the canteen, the mess and sleeping quarters while they were used for filming. In exchange for allowing their mess area to be used firefighters were given free meals on the catering bus. When a full series was commissioned, the production team built a full scale replica of the upper floor of Dockhead at Long Lane Studios in London. All exterior shots at Dockhead used the yard and the appliance bay. Because Dockhead was a busy working fire station the first priority of the film team was to make sure they were never in the way when the real fire-fighters headed out on a 'shout'. For the last two series filming switched to Leyton Fire Station in Leyton, east London.

Right: **Dockhead Fire Station the setting for *London's Burning*.**

Spooks

The first series of this long-running drama from Kudos was screened by the BBC in 2002 and became an instant hit, going on to win a BAFTA. Set among a team of M15 intelligence officers at Thames House in London, hence the term *'Spooks,'* many of the gripping episodes have been so close to the bone that at one stage, the writers or producers were believed to have links to the real intelligence service. Peter Firth, Matthew MacFadyen, Keeley Hawes, David Oyelowo and Jenny Agutter starred in the initial six-part series and now, seven series and more episodes per season later, Peter Firth is the only remaining original cast member.

Freemason's Hall in Great Queen Street, London which is home to the United Grand Lodge of England, doubles up as the exterior of Thames House, while the majority of internal shots in the 'Grid' where the team work together on their latest mission, are filmed on a specially constructed set on an industrial estate in Bermondsey, south east

Right: **Jo Portman (Miranda Raison) and Adam Carter (Rupert Penry-Jones) go into action in a dramatic scene in *Spooks*.**

London. Interior scenes had previously been filmed at a former university building in west London and then at Pinewood Studios. The design of the Grid is based exactly on the interior of the real Thames House. Over the years, *Spooks* has been filmed across most of London and has spilt over into surrounding counties such as Kent and Surrey where for instance, an old Ministry of Defence complex near Chertsey, doubled up as an American air force base. In another episode, a manor house in the same grounds was used as a secret hiding location for some of the characters.

Shooting in the heart of London with its huge, busy population of people and traffic is never easy but Location Manager Thomas Elgood who has worked on some episodes of the show said going the extra mile to obtain a certain look is exactly what makes *Spooks* so eminently watchable. "Filming in London is a struggle and for scenes to work you need plenty of space but *Spooks* is very popular and fortunately, people are often willing to help when asked," he said. "We take great care to get all the relevant permission from various people like Westminster Council, the police and the Royal Parks who are particularly good and geared up for filming. When you see the finished version, you're always glad you made the effort to get the permission because it's worth it."

Fans of the show may recall a major explosion at a central London hotel in one series. This was in fact staged inside Wandsworth Town Hall, while the exteriors were of the Adelphi Building close to the Strand. Incidentally, there's a small street nearby which often stands in for 10 Downing Street in various television productions. Other central London locations include Forbes House in Halkin Street, Belgravia, which doubled up as the Iranian Embassy. With its grand exterior it is perfect as the Embassy's stately entrance. Several scenes were shot all around the Albert Memorial, the Royal Albert Hall and St James Park thanks to friendly assistance from the Royal Parks which welcomes television crews. More into the city at Moorgate, a sniper in one episode is seen taking aim from a tall building within City Point. And while viewers may think they're watching certain scenes in the heart of London, they may actually have been filmed around the Old Naval College in Greenwich which with its tall Victorian buildings and pillars doubles up perfectly as the grandeur of the West End, particularly Whitehall. Clearly, on an on-going series such as *Spooks*, more and more locations are added every season and sometimes studios are required to film particular scenes. For instance, in series five, the final episode was shot at Action Underwater Studios in Basildon which required Adam Carter (played by Rupert Penry-Jones) and Ros Myers (Hermione Norris) to spend a great deal of time immersed in water.

2008 saw filming start on a *Spooks* spin-off series *Spooks: Code 9*. Set in 2013, London has been evacuated after a nuclear attack and M15 has moved in to set up field offices across the UK. Former Bradford police station The Tyrls was being used for production and filming and many scenes were shot on location across Bradford and Leeds.

Also in London

Love Soup

David Renwick's inventive comedy drama *Love Soup* stars Tamsin Greig as department store cosmetic counter manager Alice Chenery, whose struggle to find the perfect partner leads her down a path of disastrous dates and embarrassing mishaps. If the department store used for filming looks real, its because it is - it's actually House of Fraser's City branch, 68 King William Street. Because it is the City of London branch it isn't open at weekends which meant that in addition to exterior shots, the interior scenes could also be filmed there. Before she moved to London, Alice lived in Brighton and the building used to house her flat was the attractive 1930s Furze Croft apartment block in Furze Hill.

Minder

Even Arthur Daley was conned every time he went into the Winchester Club - because it was actually a studio set. But it wasn't always. In some early episodes of the popular ITV series, about the exploits of dodgy dealing Arthur Daley, an actual drinking club in Chalk Farm, north London, situated next to the tube station was used. The outside door to the Winchester Club actually belonged to a building at 2b Newburgh Road, Acton, north London - but characters are never actually seen going through it because it led into a private flat. Arthur's car lot changed location over the years but the one last used by the Minder production team was at 89 Churchfield Road, Acton. Arthur's lock-up, where he keeps all his dodgy gear, had changed since *Minder* began. For the last series it was at the rear of 7, Standard Road in north London. The pier that Arthur and Ray are always seen walking down during *Minder's* title sequence - that was Southend Pier in Essex.

Above: **Freemason's Hall in Great Queen Street, London which plays Thames House in *Spooks*.**

East Anglia

'Allo, 'Allo

Lynford

The BBC found the ideal location to play wartime France in *'Allo, 'Allo*, the popular comedy about the French resistance fighters. For Lynford Hall, at Lynford in Norfolk was designed in the neo-Gothic style along the lines of a French Chateau. It was ideal and saved the BBC the expense of using a real French location. Lynford Hall was perfect for *'Allo, 'Allo* as the front of the main part of the building was ideal to play Gestapo officer Herr Flick's headquarters and because the cobbled courtyard round the back was easily turned into fictional Novienne square, including Café Rene. The BBC production team built the front of the Café and other Novienne shops over the front of the archways. Interiors were filmed in a studio. Lynford Hall has also been used in *Dad's Army* and *You Rang M'Lord*. The sight of uniforms was nothing new to the Hall, as it had been used during both World Wars as a hospital for wounded officers. It is now a hotel and conference centre and has a licence for civil marriages. Further details on are available at www. lynfordhallhotel.co.uk

Right: **French-style country house Lynford Hall - home to Cafe Rene and Herr Flick in *'Allo, 'Allo*.**

Dad's Army

Thetford

A German invasion force would have been completely foiled if it had tried to find Walmington-on-Sea, where Captain Mainwaring led his Home Guard Platoon in the BBC comedy *Dad's Army*. For Walmington-On-Sea was supposed to be a small town on the coast in Sussex. Yet the whole series was filmed in and around the Norfolk town of Thetford. Producers were lucky from the start because the MoD agreed to allow them to use the Stanford Battle Area, a large nearby training area requisitioned by the army during the war. It was used for many scenes including the show's iconic closing credits.

Bill Pertwee, who plays Air Raid Warden Hodges, said: "We used it for a tremendous amount of locations, basically anything that involved chasing across fields like the episode with the barrage balloon, *The Day The Balloon Went Up*." The cast and crew used to stay at the Bell Hotel and at the Anchor Hotel in Thetford. The streets of the town were used for filming and The Guildhall which doubled as Walmington Town Hall in the episodes *The Captain's Car* and *Time on my Hands*. Much of the town was used including the Almshouses in Old Bury Road, which appeared in *The Face on the Poster*, Mill Lane, where the platoon march in *The Deadly Attachment*

Right: **They don't like it up 'em...the Walmington-on-Sea platoon charge.**

and Nether Row, which appeared in four episodes. *The Armoured Might of Lance Corporal Jones, Man Hunt, The Big Parade and Time on My Hands*. Thetford's Palace Cinema (now a bingo hall) featured in both *The Big Parade* and *A Soldier's Farewell*. Old Bury Road featured in *The Face on the Poster* and Mill Lane was used as the road to the harbour in the episode *The Deadly Attachment*.

The pier at Great Yarmouth was used for the episode *Menace From The Deep*, and a disused airfield near Diss was also utilised. Sherringham railway station, which is now a preserved line and part of North Norfolk Railway Company, was used for an episode called *The Royal Train*. The Norfolk Broads were used for an episode *Sons of the Sea*.

Another memorable episode, *The Two and a Half Feathers*, which saw the whole cast playing out a long desert scene, was filmed at large sandpits at Kings Lynn. Drinkstone Mill at Drinkstone, Suffolk was used for the episode *Don't Forget the Diver* and not far away is Wacton, setting for the episode *Round and Round Went The Big Wheel*. Santon Downham was the site of the bridge used in *Brain Versus Brawn* and Brandon Station was the railway station used in *The Big Parade*. A National Trust castle, Oxburgh Hall, was used as Peabody Museum in *Museum Piece*. Kilverstone doubled up as Waterloo in *A Soldier's Farewell* where Captain Mainwaring dreams he is Napoleon.

Right: **Captain Mainwaring (Arthur Lowe) and the vicar (Frank Williams) outside the Guildhall.**

Lynford Hall was used as the backdrop to the shooting range in *Wake Up Walmington*, an episode which also featured the Six Bells, a pub in Bardwell, which reappeared in the episode *Ring Dem Bells*.

Not strictly a television location, but one of interest to fans of Dad's Army is the pretty village of Chalfont St Giles in Buckinghamshire, which was used as the setting for the excellent 1971 *Dad's Army* feature film. Members of The Dad's Army Appreciation Society have staged tours of all these locations. For details see: www.dadsarmy.co.uk. See also: www.explorethetford.co.uk

Kingdom

Swaffham

The real life market town of Swaffham in Norfolk doubled up for Market Shipborough in ITV's top rated comedy drama *Kingdom*. Stephen Fry stars in the gentle series as a country solicitor, Peter Kingdom, who sets more store by human concerns than the law. Hermione Norris plays his batty, man-eating sister Beatrice while Celia Imrie, Phyllida Law and Tony Slattery are other big names which have helped make Kingdom so popular since it first hit our screens in 2006.

Stephen has actually lived a few miles outside Swaffham for many years and was delighted when the decision was taken to film in beautiful Norfolk. "When we decided on making Kingdom, I was very sure that the producers and writers should visit Swaffham and perhaps gain some inspiration from it," he has said. "I had secretly hoped that they would be so struck by the town that they would want to film there.

"All of us connected to Kingdom are grateful to the town and its hospitable people for allowing us the opportunity to make the series there. Dozens of actors, production staff and film technicians have fallen in love with the town and with this part of Norfolk." Although Market Shipborough is supposedly a coastal town, Swaffham is miles from the sea but an atmospheric soundtrack cleverly gives the impression otherwise.

Above (left): **Oakleigh House, Swaffham, which played Peter Kingdom's office** *(centre)* **St Peter's and St Paul's Church which appears in *Kingdom*** *(right)* **the cast on location.**

Scenes of the quayside and the harbour are filmed at Wells-next-the-Sea in north Norfolk while Holkham was used for beach shots. Viewers will note that they feature in the programme's opening credits.

Kingdom fans visiting Swaffham will have no trouble spotting many of the attractive landmarks featured heavily in the series, particularly the town centre. The market place is a familiar sight as is Oakleigh House which doubled up as Kingdom's office. The Market Shipborough sign actually covers up the real Swaffham town sign during filming, while the town's Greyhound Pub doubled up as The Startled Duck in the show.

Both Swaffham Methodist Church and St Peters and St Pauls Church featured as Market Shipborough's local church while Swaffham's Church Rooms became Market Shipborough's Church Rooms. Swaffham Library also popped up, somewhat appropriately, as the local library.

Even some of the local shops have got in on the action with a Break Charity Shop transformed into Tiger Lily's Sex Shop in one episode! Doves of Swaffham became a ladies clothes shop in another. Other locations used include RAF Marham in Norfolk, which became RAF Fakenheath for two days for a storyline in which Kingdom investigates an American soldier serving in the US Air Force.

Cockley Cley Hall doubled up as Aunt Auriel's house; racecourse scenes were shot at the famous Newmarket Racecourse and Queens College, Cambridge University appeared as Peter Kingdom's old college.

Swaffham in particular has enjoyed having the cast and crew of the series in their midst and the boost in tourism and trade has only benefitted the area. Many locals have taken up the opportunity to become extras and crew hands and indeed, a casting agency advertised in the local newspaper, inviting scores of supporting artists to come forward and try their hand at appearing on screen.

Others have rented out their homes for filming and now belong to the characters, at least on screen.

Kerry Ixer, Head of Locations at Screen East who helped make the filming of Kingdom run smoothly, said: "Two series have been filmed so far and a third will be underway later this year and everything has gone extremely well.

"Bearing in mind everything is shot on location, everyone has become very excited by *Kingdom* and everyone has wanted a piece of the pie. There's a big community spirit going on in the area. In Norfolk, they are especially film friendly.

"Not only can they see the benefit of the filming fees, but they can see the knock on effect in that it can only provide a valuable boost to Norfolk and particularly Swaffham. They're competing with other tourist destinations and this gives them something a little bit special."

Above: **Stephen Fry plays Peter Kingdom and is seen here on location in Swaffham**

Little Britain

Southwold

Old Haven, Darkley Noone, Troby, Sneddy, Herby and, of course, Llanddewi Brefi – they're the places where the weird and wonderful characters in the television comedy series *Little Britain* like Emily and Florence, Vicky Pollard, Lou and Andy, Dennis Waterman and Jeremy Rent, Kenny Craig and Daffyd live.

And before you think that the hit show's writers and stars David Walliams and Matt Lucas have invented names that are too wacky as to be believable, keep reading – for the following six names are real places in Britain: Bozomzeal (in Devon), Blubberhouses (Yorkshire), Clenchwarton (Norfolk), Dull (Perthshire), Pratt's Bottom (Greater London) and Ugley (Essex).

For series two of *Little Britain* Old Haven, home to those would-be ladies Emily Howard and Florence, was filmed in picturesque Southwold in Suffolk. Producer Geoff Posner told the local paper *The East Anglian Daily Times*: "It's perfect for Emily and Florence, the failed transvestites, who have a somewhat Victorian air about them - like Southwold!"

For the third series Eastbourne, East Sussex played the town and holiday makers out for a stroll were faced with two men dressed as women enjoying a ride on a carousel and the sight of Matt Lucas dressed as a baby. This time Posner told *Eastbourne Today* newspaper: "'The characters Emily and Florence live in a Victorian world and the architecture of Eastbourne fits their world completely."

Scenes supposed to be Troby, where Lou and Andy live, have been filmed in various locations. For the third series a scene where Andy hops out of his wheelchair and joined

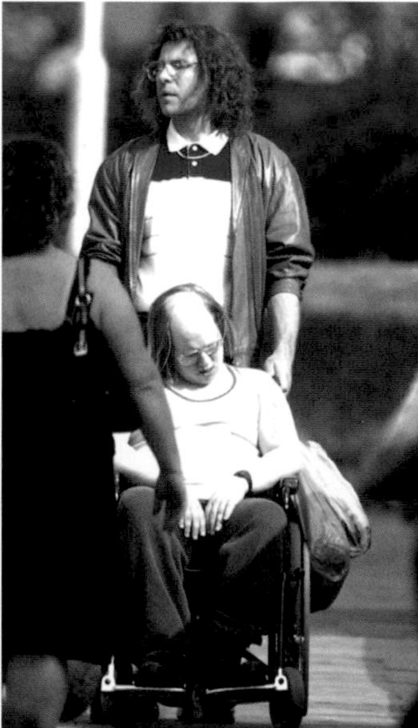

Right: **David Walliams and Matt Lucas film scenes from the outrageous but hilarious *Little Britain*.**

Above: **Emily (David Walliams) and Florence (Matt Lucas) enjoying a carousel in Eastbourne.**

in a rugby match when Lou isn't watching was filmed London Skolars New River Stadium in White Hart Lane, London. Another sketch, when Andy does a parachute jump, was filmed at RAF Hendon, north London. Other scenes were shot in Notting Hill, London.

Scenes of Lou and Andy's home have been filmed on the Cranbrook Estate in Bethnal Green, London and the scene where Andy buys a snake was shot at a real pet shop, Magri's Pets at 205 Roman Road, also in Bethnal Green. Bubbles Devere keeps that fabulous shape by spending lots of time at Hill Grange Health Spa in Trump, scenes for which were filmed at Gaddesden Place in Hemel Hempstead, headquarters of computer software company Xara. Gaddesden Place is a veteran location and has been in many films and television series including *Sharpe*, *Jeeves and Wooster*, *Jonathan Creek*, *Lewis* and *Foyle's War*.

The very striking former Royal Masonic School building in Bushey, Hertfordshire was used as Kelsey Grammar School, where Mr Cleaves teaches, and it has also been used many times for films including *The Meaning of Life* and on television for *Inspector Morse*, *Hex* and *My Dad's The Prime Minister*. The building is now being converted into luxury apartments. Daffyd's village of Llandewi Breffi is spelt differently from the real village of Llandewi Brefi (which has only one 'f') in west Wales. There have been reports of attempted theft of village signs even though no scenes have actually been filmed there.

Lovejoy

Long Melford

You might not bump into that loveable rogue Lovejoy if you head to Long Melford in Suffolk but you will find scores of genuine antique shops full of the sort of stuff Lovejoy would love to get his hands on.

Long Melford, so named because of its particularly long high street, which is three miles long, was one of around a dozen in Suffolk regularly used for filming *Lovejoy*, the highly successful BBC series which stars Ian McShane as the eponymous antique dealer. The attractive 16th Century Bull Hotel was regularly featured in the series along with many of the village's antique shops including Neptune Antiques and Ringer's Yard.

Over at Belchamp Walter, opposite the beautiful 15th Century village church with medieval wall paintings, is Belchamp Hall, an elegant Queen Anne redbrick house, which was used as Lady Jane's home, Felsham Hall, in the series. The Hall is also available for hire for conferences, weddings and parties and the converted stables can be rented for holidays and short breaks. For more details go to www.belchamphall.com

Above (left): **Belchamp Hall, which played Lady Jane's home** *(right)* **Ian McShane as *Lovejoy***

The attractive 300-year-old thatched Half Moon pub at nearby Belchamp St Paul was a familiar sight in the Autumn 1993 series of *Lovejoy* when it becomes one of his locals. Elsewhere many other towns and villages in the area were regularly used in the series including Braintree, Hadleigh, Kersey, Lavenham, Felsham, Sudbury, Halstead, Bildeston and Bury St Edmunds and all are interesting places to visit in addition to being *Lovejoy* filming locations.

Martin Chuzzlewit

King's Lynn

Written in 1843, *Martin Chuzzlewit* was Charles Dickens' sixth novel, and filming requirements called for a labyrinth of tiny streets, supposedly in early 19th Century London. The BBC found the perfect location in the attractive Norfolk town of King's Lynn.

The story centres on an inheritance and the contrasting destinies of the wealthy brothers Chuzzlewit and features an all-star cast including Sir John Mills, Paul Schofield, Keith Allen, Tom Wilkinson and Julia Sawalha.

King's Lynn was one of England's foremost ports as early as the 12th Century and even today late medieval merchants' houses stretch back to the river between cobbled lanes and the famous Custom House.

Above: **Peckover House in Cambridgeshire played Montague Tigg's home.**

Those tiny streets proved to be perfect for the production team and where there were modern road markings mud was used cover them up. King's Lynn Council's offices doubled as Mrs Todgers' boarding houses and the frontages of cottages at King's Straithe, which also played early New York in the film *Revolution*, were used extensively.

Elsewhere, St Margaret's House and the lane next door appeared, as did the back of King's Street. "King's Lynn offered us the labyrinth of tiny streets that Dickens mentions in the novel," said Production Designer Gavin Davies. "I could get seven important locations within 10 minutes of one another.

"Doing it in London would have been difficult if not downright impossible because of noise and traffic. We were able to close roads in King's Lynn without disrupting the whole town."

Elsewhere, The Fleece Inn, a 14th Century pub in the Worcestershire Village of Bretforton, appeared as The Blue Dragon and a National Trust property, Peckover House in Cambridgeshire, played Montague Tigg's home. See www.nationaltrust.org.uk for further details.

Honington Hall, a 17th Century house at Shipston-on-Stour, Warwickshire, also appeared. The house, which has also featured in *Our Mutual Friend* and *Keeping Up Appearances*, is open to the public at certain times. For further details telephone: 01608 661434.

The Mill on the Floss

Bintree

The BBC's 1997 adaptation of *The Mill on the Floss,* George Eliot's classic tale of unrequited love which stars Emily Watson, James Frain and Bernard Hill, who went on to play Captain Smith in the blockbuster film *Titanic*, featured a number of stunning locations.

Above: **Bintree Mill, the main setting for *The Mill on the Floss.***

To find the principal location, that of the Dorlcote Mill, Location Manager Jeremy Johns visited 50 water-mills all over the country from Devon to the Lake District and from Wales to East Anglia. "The main criteria was that it had to be picturesque with as few modern additions as possible.

"From a short-list of three mills in Norfolk, Warwickshire and Dorset, we finally decided upon Bintree Mill in Norfolk which was a real find," he recalled. "It was ideal because it is set in a green belt valley with very few telephone and electricity cables, rather than in the middle of a village.

"When we found most of the film's other settings and locations in the vicinity, Bintree was a winner," added Jeremy. The interiors of Dorlcote – the corn-loft, milling-floor and sack chute – were found in another mill 16 miles away in Burgh-next-Aylsham and the kitchen and parlour interiors were filmed in an old farmhouse in Salle. Nearby were the locations for Lawyer Wakem's house and Lucy Deane's house, while the flood and rowing scenes were shot on a lake near Bintree.

Also in East Anglia

Hi-De-Hi

The BBC comedy *Hi-De-Hi,* set in a 1950s holiday camp, was another huge hit from the script-writing partnership of Jimmy Perry and David Croft. It was popular with the public but holiday giants Butlins were less than impressed and refused to let the BBC use one of their holiday camps for filming. They had spent years, not to mention thousands of pounds in advertising, trying to shake off the old-fashioned holiday camp image which *Hi-De-Hi* recreated.

Another company, Warners, had no such objections to the show and allowed the BBC to film at their holiday camp at Dovercourt, near Frinton-on-Sea. Filming began at the camp a week after the last campers left, either the last week in September or the first week of October. By that time the weather had usually begun to get chilly and the cast would frequently complain about the cold. It was bulldozed several years ago to make way for a housing estate, although the holiday tradition lives on nearby as there is a section for touring caravans at the nearby Dovercourt Caravan Park.

The Midlands

By The Sword Divided

Market Harborough

Location managers could hardly have found a better location than Rockingham Castle for the BBC's 1983 series By *The Sword Divided*. Set in 1640 during the English Civil War, the series follows the lives of the Royalist Lacey family and documents their involvement in the conflict. It stars Julian Glover as Sir Martin Lacey, Sharon Maughan as his daughter Anne Lacey, and Timothy Bentinck, famous on radio as David Archer in *The Archers*, as his son Tom Lacey, and ran for two 10-part series.

Rockingham was perfect as Arnescote because it had real life experiences of the Civil War when it was badly damaged, having had its Norman keep razed to the ground, its walls pocked by cannon and its pleasure gardens flattened. Rockingham has been in the Watson family since 1530. The first Lord Rockingham, Sir Lewis Watson, was a Royalist, but his wife Eleanor was a Parliamentarian. However, they agreed on one subject - that their home, with its keep and fortress wall which commanded views over four counties was bound to be occupied by soldiers.

Above: **Stunning Rockingham Castle, still owned by the same family for nearly 500 years.**

They expected Royalists to occupy Rockingham and Parliamentary forces to take nearby Belvoir Castle. Based on this theory they sent their gold and silver to Belvoir for safe-keeping. But Belvoir fell to the Royalists and Rockingham to the Parliamentarians. So the Watsons lost their property and valuables to both factions and Sir Lewis was first imprisoned by the Royalists for disloyalty, then fined £5,000 by the Commonwealth.

Charles Dickens was a frequent visitor during the 19th Century and he wrote a large portion of his novel *Bleak House* during his stays at the castle. More than three centuries after the Civil War, Rockingham, which is still owned by the Watson family, saw Cavalier and Roundhead battles again when the BBC arrived. The film team added mock stone castellations, disguised post-Commonwealth features and covered modern roads with mushroom compost, but other than these superficial changes, Arnescote is Rockingham and what we first saw on television more than two decades ago can be seen now. Rockingham Castle, which is licenced for civil weddings, is open to the public throughout the summer on certain days of the week. See www.rockinghamcastle.com for details. In addition, visitors can see the castle at other times during the year by appointment.

Dangerfield

Warwick

The BBC drama, which stars Nigel Havers as police surgeon Dr Jonathan Paige and Jane Gurnett as Detective Inspector Gillian Cramer, was filmed in and around the beautiful town of Warwick, which is dominated by magnificent Warwick Castle. The key location for the show is Dr Paige's surgery and if it looks authentic that was because it was, as the exterior scenes were filmed at a real-life surgery, The Old Dispensary in Castle Street, Warwick.

The first four series of the show feature Nigel Le Vaillant as Dr Paul Dangerfield and his home for the first three series was played by a house on Shipston Road near Stratford Upon Avon. For series four he moved to another house, played by The Malt House in Mill Street, Warwick. The house that played Dr Paige's home was in Castle Street, Warwick. For the first four series the real life police stations at Leamington Spa and Warwick doubled as the police station but regular noise interruptions to filming meant a new location, the front of the Heart of England Building Society, Castle Lane, was used for the fifth series. St Mary's Church in the centre of Warwick was used for the wedding of Dr Dangerfield's daughter Alison.

All the interior shots for the police station, the surgery, Dr Paige's home and the mortuary were filmed on specially built sets in an industrial unit at Redditch. The production team used to use the real-life mortuary at Warwick Hospital but they could only film there after 4.30pm on a Friday, which was inconvenient, and the film crew apparently couldn't stand the smell!

Right: **Stunning Lord Leycester Hospital in Warwick, the town where the BBC drama *Dangerfield* was filmed.**

Inspector Morse

Oxford

There is very little of central Oxford that hasn't, at some time, appeared in *Inspector Morse*, the award-winning detective series which stars the late John Thaw as the thoughtful Oxford sleuth. Some landmarks are easily recognisable from the television, but others, notably the colleges, are more difficult because often several different real locations were used to make one fictional place.

The King's Arms, known as the KA, on the corner of Hollywell Street and Parks Road, is one of the easily identifiable places - and is used by Morse to down a few pints of his favourite Samuel Smith's best bitter in several episodes. Just along in Holywell Street is the Music Room, owned by Wadham College, which was used in the 1993 episode *Twilight of the Gods* when opera singer Gladys Probert, played by the late Sheila Gish, gives a masterclass.

Back in Broad Street is the bookshop, Blackwells, where Morse is seen in several episodes buying books, and next door is the White Horse pub, another location where Morse can often be found drinking. On the other side of Broad Street is the impressive Sheldonian Theatre, where Oxford University confers its degrees. In *Inspector Morse* it was used in the episode *Dead on Time* when Morse takes his ex-fiancee Susan Fallon to a concert there.

Below: **A stunning rooftop view of All Souls College.**

Above: **John Thaw and Kevin Whately pictured outside the imposing Radcliffe Camera, Oxford.**

To the side of the Sheldonian Theatre, next door to the Bodleian Library lies the square used for *Twilight of The Gods* where a shooting takes place. In Radcliffe Square, not far from Broad Street, is the unusually shaped Radcliffe Camera and next door to it is Brasenose College which appeared as two fictional colleges Beaufort and Beaumont in various episodes.

Seen from the beautiful Christchurch meadow is Merton College which appeared in the episode *The Infernal Serpent*. Christchurch itself was used as the backdrop to several episodes, and is very noticeable because of its distinctive Tom Tower. The porter's lodge at Pembroke College was used for the episode *Deceived By Flight* when Sergeant Robbie Lewis (Kevin Whately) poses as a porter to catch a murderer and a smuggler. "I think we filmed at every college in Oxford that would have us," said Location Manager Russell Lodge. "And that was 90 per cent of them."

Out of the city at Wolvercote is the delightful Trout pub which is on the bank of the River Isis. It was from the bridge next to the pub that Morse and Lewis watched a frogman recover the Anglo-Saxon belt buckle, the Wolvercote Tongue, in the episode of the same name. The Randolph Hotel in Beaumont Street was also featured heavily in the episode and also appears in other stories. It was also regularly used by John Thaw when he stayed in Oxford for filming and appeared in the film *Shadowlands*. Oxford wasn't the only place used to film *Morse* - in the episode *Masonic Mysteries* none of the city was used. Although on screen it looks like Morse rarely leaves Oxford, usually only five days of filming out of 25 are done in the city, with the rest of the days shot in other locations doubling as Oxford.

A territorial army centre in Southall, London, was used as the police station for the first two series, although for those series the front we see on screen was the front of the real Oxford police station. For the third, fourth and fifth series a TA centre in Harrow played the police station and a Ministry of Defence laboratory in Harefield in Hertfordshire did the same job in the sixth and seventh series, but was demolished in the spring of 1993.

The front of the police station was not shown that much on screen as *Morse* and *Lewis* mainly used the back entrance. Morse's home is actually miles from Oxford. It is a ground floor flat in a Victorian block in Castlebar Road, Ealing. When Morse's home caught fire in one episode a set of the flat was built in a studio and burned, although fake smoke came through a broken window at the actual flat too. It was filmed in Ealing because it was cheaper not to travel to Oxford as it didn't involve an expensive overnight stay for the actors and crew. Many of the streets in Ealing look very similar to houses on the Woodstock or Banbury roads out of Oxford.

Stately homes were also often prominent in *Morse* including Cornbury Park in Chalbury, Oxfordshire, which was used for the episode *Greeks Bearing Gifts*, Englefield House, near Reading, which had also been used for *Jeeves and Wooster* and the mini-series *A Woman of Substance*, appeared in *Twilight of The Gods* and 14th Century Shirburn Castle, was used for the 1994 episode *Happy Families*.

Above: **An aerial view of Magdelen College and Bridge.**

Another of Morse's favourite pubs, which was supposed to be near Oxford, was actually filmed at The Crown at Bray in Berkshire. "We used the inside a lot," said Russell Lodge. "We slightly decorated the inside by changing the pictures, and they are still up now." The pub was picked because the Morse production team were filming at nearby Bray film studios. The 1998 episode *The Wench Is Dead*, which saw actor Matthew Finney joining Morse as his new sidekick Adrian Kershaw instead of Lewis, was filmed at The Black Country Museum at Dudley and on canals in Northamptonshire and Wiltshire.

The graveyard scenes – supposedly in Ireland – were filmed at Abersoch in Wales and a few extra fibreglass gravestones were added to real ones there. Morse spends most of the episode in Radcliffe Infirmary in Oxford and the scenes of him leaving were actually filmed there. The Radcliffe appeared again in the final episode of Inspector Morse, *The Remorseful Day*, which was first broadcast on November 15th 2000, as did the Randolph Hotel where Morse has coffee with Dr Harrison. Morse and Lewis meet for their last pint at the Victoria Arms in Mill Lane Old Marston and at the end of the episode Morse collapses and dies of a heart attack in the quadrangle of Exeter College in Turl Street.

Keeping Up Appearances

Coventry

The Coventry suburb of Binley Woods was the fictional home of social-climbing Hyacinth Bucket (or Bouquet as she pronounces it) and her put upon husband Richard, in the hit BBC comedy series *Keeping Up Appearances*. The owners of 117 Heather Road, which doubled up as the exterior of the Bucket residence, thought it was a joke when a location manager first asked if the BBC could use the house for filming as they did not know that their neighbours at Number 119 had already agreed to let the BBC use their home as the Bucket's neighbours Elizabeth and Emmet's house.

Before filming began the production team used to put a fake garden to the side of the garage, extra plants to the existing flower border and add extra net curtains so the occupants couldn't be seen during filming outside. Patricia Routledge, who plays Hyacinth, used the house's dining room as her make-up room but the interior scenes were filmed later at BBC studios. A few miles away, on a council estate in the Stoke district of Coventry, is Michell Close where Number Three played the home of Hyacinth's brother Onslow and his wife Daisy. The house was chosen because there is a scrapyard at the end of the road which was used as Onslow's yard.

Lewis

Oxford

Not even Kevin Whately who plays the unsophisticated Lewis believed he'd ever reprise the role he played for 13 years as Morse's sidekick in ITV's popular police drama *Inspector Morse*. After the death of Morse and of course his alter ego, the late John Thaw, it was difficult to imagine the detective ever returning to our screens without his boss and mentor telling him what to do.

Yet six years after Chief Inspector Morse died of a heart attack, Lewis, now promoted to Detective Inspector Lewis, returned in 2006 doing what he does best – solving murders in the academic world of Oxford – with his own sidekick, Detective Sergeant James Hathaway, played by Laurence Fox. His return, first in a pilot episode then a full series, delighted fans, not just because writer Colin Dexter's tales are always so absorbing but because it gave them a chance to revisit all those Oxford haunts which helped make Inspector Morse so enjoyable to watch. Indeed, Oxford is a favoured town for many a location manager and has featured in the *Harry Potter* films, *Shadowlands*, *Midsomer Murders* and *Brideshead Revisited* to name but a few other productions.

Below: **Laurence Fox as Detective Sergeant James Hathaway and Kevin Whately as Detective Inspector Robert Lewis, the stars of *Lewis*.**

Many Oxford colleges including Wadham in Parks Road, Trinity, Brasenose and Lincoln which featured as Lonsdale College in series two, Exeter and Hertford Colleges can be spotted in several episodes of Lewis, with often just the exteriors of these beautiful

buildings used to double up for other venues. Corpus Christi College was used in episode one of series two and the crew were even allowed to film a scene on a roof that was under construction. In that same episode, filming also took place at New College and University College where the Shelley Memorial is based.

"During the holidays most colleges are available for filming although two or three of them are unfortunately too expensive for television drama," said Nick Marshall who was Location Manager on series two of *Lewis*. "All the colleges we filmed at were very accommodating towards us. But on the other hand, nobody loses sight of the fact that the education of the students is the most important thing and we did find that once university holidays were over, we couldn't always film at certain colleges.

"Fortunately, Trinity allowed us to film for three and a half days during term time which was a great help." The well-kept grounds of virtually every Oxford college are ideal backdrops for Lewis and Hathaway, who are often seen strolling them while discussing their latest case.

Of course the distinguished, wood-panelled interiors of some of the colleges are also used in certain episodes. For instance, in *Old School Ties*, screened in 2007, the inside of Caroline's (Emma Campbell Webster) college room was shot at Merton College in Merton Street, while the porter's lodge of her college was filmed at Oriel College in Oriel Street.

The Principal's house of Hertford College also doubled up as the home of a character in episode four of series two. Nick was particularly delighted to receive permission to film at Oxford's renowned Bodleian Library in Broad Street which is the main library of the University of Oxford and is open to the public. In fact the library's Divinity Room and Exhibition room attract over 200,000 visitors a year.

"We did quite a lot at The Bodleian Library," said Nick, "particularly, and uniquely, in the basement and amongst the basement stacks, where a great many old and precious books are kept." For further information on the library, go to www.bodley.ox.ac.uk During the very early days of *Morse*, the production would be based in the centre of the city by the Radcliffe Camera until permission was withdrawn. This is exactly where *Lewis* was based during filming of the pilot and first series, much to the delight of the production team. For series two, the unit base was situated at the car park of Oxpens Coach Park by the ice rink while Radcliffe Square was used to park essential equipment vehicles nearer to the centre of Oxford.

"The Police and the Council were most welcoming when I told them we were planning to return for another series, and were extremely helpful throughout," says Nick. There is of course more to Oxford than simply its seats of academia with the town centre itself, restaurants, hotels and stunning Botanic Garden in Rose Lane also featuring in *Lewis*. The Garden was established in 1621 making it the oldest botanic garden in the UK and the third oldest in the world. With thousands of species of plants, a magnificent greenhouse and walled section, it is a popular tourist attraction and well worth a visit. Telephone 01865 286690 to find out about opening times.

Fans of the show will recall seeing the Bridge of Sighs in more than one episode. This is to be found in New College Lane and its official name is Hertford Bridge. The reason it is commonly referred to as the Bridge of Sighs is because of its strong resemblance to the

Above: **The beautiful Radcliffe Camera in Oxford.**

bridge of the same name in Venice. It was designed by Sir Thomas Jackson, finished in 1914 and links the old and new quadrangles of Hertford College.

If you're planning a visit to the city, why not stop for a drink at the Turf Tavern tucked away in Bath Place which with foundations linking back to the 14th Century, makes it the oldest pub in Oxford. Lewis and Hathaway can be seen enjoying a drink there in one episode, although the pair don't have a regular social haunt. If you do pop in, look out for the sketch of *Inspector Morse* on the wall. The Ashmolean Museum of Art and Archaeology features in *Lewis* on more than one occasion. Situated in Beaumont Street, it was founded in 1683 and is one of the oldest public museums in the world, offering a variety of exhibitions throughout the year and better still, no entry fee. Go to www.ashmolean.org for further information.

To the north west of Oxford is an area called Jericho consisting of rows and rows of terrace houses. Locals may recognise the area when they tune into repeats of *Lewis*, in particular Nelson Street where a large explosion was staged for one episode. Of course, not all scenes in *Lewis* were filmed in Oxford at all. For instance, West Car Park at Slough Railway Station doubled up as Oxford Railway Station in at least one scene while The Duke of Kent, Scotch Common in Ealing doubled up as an Oxford restaurant in an episode where Lewis has dinner with Diane Turnbull, played by Gina McKee. The old DHSS office in Ealing has been used for various interiors and Lewis' own flat is actually filmed in a property in Ealing while Hathaway's flat is in Shepherds Bush, west London.

Middlemarch

Stamford

Producers of the 1994 BBC serial *Middlemarch*, which stars Rufus Sewell as Will Ladislaw, Douglas Hodge as Tertius Lydgate and Juliet Aubrey as Dorothea Brooke, quite expected to have to film in many different towns in order to authentically recreate Victorian England. Virtually nowhere exists unaltered since the 1830s as Producer Louis Marks explained: "We presumed we'd have to film all over the country - a street here, a square there, a house somewhere else.

"But then our researchers came back and told us they'd found this marvellous town that had everything. So I went up to Lincolnshire, took one look and I knew they were right. Stamford is beautiful."

The town needed some ageing so period-style doors were placed over new ones and Georgian-type windows were hung over the top of modern ones. Locations used in the town include unspoiled St George's Square, Browne's Hospital and the area Barn Hill - which includes Number Three All Saints Place, which played Doctor Lydgate's home.

Outside the town centre Grimsthorpe Castle doubled as Qualingham. The castle, which was also used for scenes in *Moll Flanders* and *The Buccaneers*, is open to the public for much of the year. See www.grimsthorpe.co.uk for details.

The opening episode carriage scenes were filmed in Burghley Park. The Park is open all year and 16th Century Elizabethan Burghley House is open for much of the year. See www.burghley.co.uk for details.

Rambling Mill Lane and Stamford Arts Centre, which doubled as the White Hart Hotel, also appear. In fact the Arts Centre, which also contains Stamford Tourist Information Centre, looked so much like a hotel after the BBC film team decorated it that several visitors to the town during filming tried to book rooms!

Right (top): **Rufus Sewell as Will Ladislaw in *Middlemarch* and** *(bottom)* **Stamford, the main location for the 1994 BBC adaptation.**

In 2004 the building, along with St George's Square and St Mary's Street,was used for the film version of *Pride and Prejudice*, which stars Keira Knightley and Matthew Macfadyen. This time the town played the village of Meryton, home to the Bennet family.

Peak Practice

Crich

Peak Practice became one of ITV's most successful drama series of the 90s. It began in 1993 starring Kevin Whately as Dr Jack Kerruish, Amanda Burton as Dr Beth Glover and Simon Shepherd as Dr Will Preston as the GPs at The Beeches surgery in the fictional village of Cardale. Over the years characters changed but it continued to be successful and ran until 2002. The pretty Derbyshire village of Crich played Cardale and fans of the show can easily find plenty of locations. Even before you reach Crich marketplace you'll spot on your left, down the hill next to the Black Swan pub, Archway House that played Dr Beth Glover's home.

Next you'll see the Costcutter shop which doubled as the bank in the series and a few doors along from that is the local fish and chip shop which is now called The Cardale Fish and Chip Shop in honour of the series. The series' cast and crew often visited the shop while filming and Kevin Whately used to be a regular. To find the house that played Dr Kerruish's home take a left turn down Dimple lane, go down for about a quarter of a mile until you see fields on your left, carry on further and you'll find private Melkridge House that played his home.

Returning to the main road turn left at the top of Dimple Lane and follow the road for about a mile until you see a sign marked Fritchley 1/4 of a mile. Follow the sign and go down the hill until you find Bobbin Mill Hill. Go down Bobbin Mill Hill and up on a sharp right hand bend is Chesnut Bank House, a large private house, which played The Beeches surgery in the series. The pub where Jack Kerruish gets involved in a fight in an early episode of Peak Practice is actually The Manor Hotel, in nearby South Wingfield. Nearby Wingfield Manor, a ruined mansion now owned by English Heritage was used for Cardale's mediaeval pageant. For further details about the house, which was also used for Franco Zeffirelli's 1996 film *Jane Eyre* see www.englishheritage.org.uk

The church where Dr Erica Matthews jilts Dr Andrew Attwood during the 1998 series was St Peter's Church at Edensor inside Chatsworth Park. Dr David Shearer is hit and killed by a motorcycle at Elton and the funeral was filmed at St Giles Church at Hartington. Outside Crich locations all round the Peak District and in the magnificent Peak District National Park were regularly used.

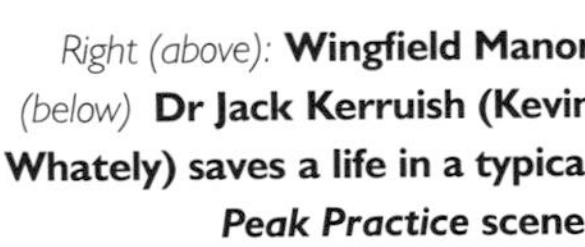

Right (above): **Wingfield Manor** *(below)* **Dr Jack Kerruish (Kevin Whately) saves a life in a typical *Peak Practice* scene.**

Vanity Fair

Warwickshire

Set during the Napoleonic Wars, William Makepeace Thackeray's classic novel *Vanity Fair* follows the life of Becky Sharp, the penniless, orphaned daughter of an artist and a French opera dancer and Amelia Sedley, the sheltered child of a rich city merchant. They make a pair of unlikely but firm friends who are very different in character. Becky is an irresistible schemer and will stop at nothing to get what she wants whereas Amelia is meek and mild.

The lavish 1998 BBC adaptation of *Vanity Fair* stars Natasha Little as Becky, Frances Grey as Amelia, Nathaniel Parker as red-blooded Rawdon Crawley and Tom Ward as dashing officer George Osborne.

The series took 21 weeks to film and was shot in locations as diverse as London, Paris, the Rhine Valley and the coast of west Wales. The Ballroom scene was filmed at Cheltenham Town Hall and the town's Pittville Pump Room was used as a foreign restaurant for another scene. Both are open to the public and part of the Pump Room is now a museum.

The beach and several rows of houses in Tenby, Wales doubled as Brighton and Ragley Hall, Warwickshire, played the home of Lord Steyne. Claydon House at Middle Claydon, Buckinghamshire also featured, playing the interior of a hotel in Germany. It is owned by the National Trust and is open to the public as is Stowe Landscape Gardens at Buckingham, Buckinghamshire, a stunning survivor of Georgian times whch doubled as Hyde Park. See www.nationaltrust.org.uk

Below: **Two views of stunning Stowe Landscape Gardens, used as Hyde Park, London in *Vanity Fair***

Wales

Doctor Who

Since its return in 2005 *Doctor Who* has been a huge success for the BBC - and a fantastic boost for the city of Cardiff where the show is produced. The production team has been very inventive and locations all over the city and in the wider area have been used to play both places on earth and further afield. The following list provides details of many of the key places used for filming.

The Ninth Doctor - Christopher Eccleston

Series One (2005)

Rose

Howells department store (Henrik's department store), University Hospital of Wales (Henrik's basement), La Fosse restaurant (Tizano's restaurant), Cardiff Royal Infirmary (restaurant yard), Queen's Arcade, Working Street (shopping centre) disused Ely Papermill Grangetown (Nestene's lair), Flats at Lydstep Crescent, Gabalfa (all Cardiff), Royal Air Force memorial, Embankment, London.

Above and below: **Christopher Eccleston and Billie Piper filming scenes for *The Unquiet Dead* in Swansea.**

The End of The World

Temple of Peace Hall (reception area), BBC Broadcasting House, Churchill Way (corridors) both in Cardiff

The Unquiet Dead

White Swan Court (Tardis lands), Beaufort Arms Court, Monmouth (outside of Sneed's undertakers), New Theatre, Cardiff (theatre), The Exchange Building, Swansea (theatre exterior), Headland School, Penarth (chapel of rest), Cambrian Place, Swansea (street)

Aliens of London

Cardiff Royal Infirmary (Albion Hospital), Hensol Castle, Vale of Glamorgan (inside Downing Street). John Adam Street, London (Downing Street), Westminster Bridge and Tower Bridge, London (themselves),

World War III

John Adam Street, London (Downing Street), Brandon Estate, Kennington, London (Tardis crashes), Lower Dock Street, Newport (the remains of Downing Street), Hensol Castle, Vale of Glamorgan (inside Downing Street)

Dalek

Corridors and staircase under Millennium Stadium, Cardiff

The Long Game

Filmed in a studio

Above: **Billie Piper as seen in *The Idiot's Lantern*.**

Father's Day

Office at ITV Wales (register office), St Paul's Church, Grangetown (church), Loudoun Square, Butetown, Cardiff (Pete is run over), Paget Street, Grangetown (street), St Fagan's Street, Cardiff (Tardis lands)

The Empty Child

Headlands School, Penarth (nightclub), Cardiff Royal Infirmary (Albion Hospital), Barry Island railway www.valeofglamorganrailway.co.uk (railway station), Womanby Street (Street)

The Doctor Dances

See The Empty Child

Boom Town

Roald Dahl Plass, Cardiff Bay (Tardis lands), Glamorgan Building, Cardiff University (city hall), The Bosphorous, Cardiff Bay, (restaurant). Other scenes filmed at Mermaid Quay and Cardiff Central station.

Bad Wolf

Flat at Severn Square, Cardiff (Big Brother House),

The Parting of the Ways

Loudoun Square, Butetown, Cardiff (the Tyler's estate), Paddle Steamer Cafe, Loudoun Square (chip shop), playground at Canal Park, Butetown.

The Tenth Doctor - David Tennant

The Christmas Invasion

Howells department store (Henrik's department store), Millennium Stadium loading areas (UNIT HQ). Baltic House in Mount Stuart Square, Cardiff (fire escape), British Gas Building, Tredegar House, Newport – open to the public (Downing Street interior), Clearwell Caves, Gloucestershire www.clearwellcaves.com (Sycorax spaceship interior), Barry Docks (Sycorax spaceship), Tower of London (UNIT HQ exterior)

Series Two (2006)

New Earth

Worm's Head at Rhossili - Gower Peninsula (Rose and the Doctor admire New Earth), Wales Millennium Centre, Cardiff Bay (alien Hospital), Tredegar House, Newport (basement), disused Ely Papermill, Cardiff (testing lab), Ba Orient, Cardiff Bay (nightclub)

Tooth and Claw

Gelligaer Common, Fochriiw, Merthyr (Tardis lands), Craig-Y-Nos Castle, Brecon Beacons - www.craigynoscastle.com (Sir Robert's House), Penllyn Castle, Cowbridge (courtyard), Headland School, Penarth (corridor), Tredegar House, Newport (various interiors)

School Reunion
Belle View Park (Tardis lands), Duffryn High School, Newport (school), Fitzalan High School, Canton, Cardiff (school), Da Vinci's Coffee Shop, High Street, Newport (coffee shop), Belle Vue Park, Newport (Doctor says farewell to Sarah Jane)

The Girl in the Fireplace
Dyffryn Gardens, Vale of Glamorgan - www.dyffryngardens.org.uk (Palace of Versailles), Ragley Hall, Alcester - www.ragleyhall.com (Versailles ballroom)

Rise of the Cybermen
Riverfront Arts Centre, Newport (Tardis arrives), South Side Roath Dock, Cardiff Docks (recruitment area), Cardiff Heliport (President's arrival), Mount Stuart Square, Cardiff Bay (street), Sanatorium Road, Cardiff (army checkpoint), Compton Street, Grangetown (Mickey snatched), Coedarhydyglyn House, near Cardiff – private residence (the Tyler home), Lambeth Pier, Albert Embankment, London (Tardis arrives)

The Age of Steel
Newport Docks (Cybermen give chase), Grangemoor Park (making plans scene), Magor Brewery, Bridgend (humans converted), Uskmouth Power Station (Cyberfactory)

The Idiot's Lantern
Shop in Blenheim Road, Cardiff (Magpie Electricals), Florentia Street (Florizel Street), South Dock, Newport Docks (Bishop's HQ), Cardiff Royal Infirmary (Alexandra Palace), Cardiff Heliport (top of transmitter),

The Impossible Planet
Mamhilad Park Industrial Estate, Pontypool (Ood holding pens), Wenvoe Quarry, Cardiff (planet surface),

The Satan Pit
Clearwell Caves in Gloucestershire (The Satan Pit),

Above: **The Doctor (David Tennant) in fine voice and** *(below)* **Billie Piper makes a suprise appearance in *Partners In Crime*.**

Love & Monsters
Cargo Road, Cardiff Docks (Woolwich), Impounding station, Newport Docks (Elton tries to find the Doctor), Heol Pentwyn, Cardiff (Elton's home), The Hayes, Cardiff (London shopping street). Llandaff Fields, Cardiff (Elton meets Ursula). Jacob's Antiques, West Canal Wharf (Ll'n'DA headquarters), St David's Market, Cardiff (looking for Jackie), Adam Street Car Park (The Doctor meets the Abzorbaloff), St. Peter's Sport and Social Club, Minster Road, Cardiff (Elton and his mother)

Fear Her
Page Drive, Cardiff (Kelly Holmes Close) Storage Yard. Newport Road, Cardiff (East London), Millennium Stadium (Olympic Stadium) in Cardiff, St Alban's Rugby Club (Doctor light's torch)

Army of Ghosts
St Mary Street (Rose on bus), Southerndown beach, Ogmore Vale, Vale of Glamorgan (alien world), Brandon Estate , Kennington, London (Powell Estate), Loudoun Square, Cardiff (Tyler estate), aircraft hanger RAF St Athlan (Torchwood), Brackla Bunkers,

Bridgend (Torchwood corridors), Broadstairs Road, Cardiff (Cybermen attack house), One Canada Square, London (Torchwood Tower), Compass Bridge Road, Cardiff Docks (battle)

Doomsday
See *Army of Ghosts*, plus: Broadstairs Road, Cardiff (Cybermen march), Coedarhydyglyn House, near Cardiff – private residence (the Tyler home), Southerndown beach, Ogmore Vale, Vale of Glamorgan (Doctor and Rose says goodbye)

The Runaway Bride
St John the Baptist at Trinity Street, Cardiff (St Mary's Church, Chiswick), Churchill Way, Cardiff (Tardis lands), Old Library, The Hayes, Cardiff (evil santas), Wall next to Waterstones, Wharton Street, Cardiff (cashpoint), A4232 at Leckwith and Great West Road, Chiswick (Tardis chase), Atradius, Cardiff Bay (Donna's workplace). Baverstock Hotel, Merthyr Tydfil (Evil santas invade wedding reception - interior), New Country House Hotel, Thornhill, Cardiff (wedding reception – exterior), Millennium Stadium (Tardis lands underground), Impound station, Newport Docks (the empress's lair), St Mary Street, Cardiff (tank), International Press Centre, Shoe Lane, London (rooftop), Princes Avenue, Cardiff (Donna's parents home)

Below: **The Doctor (David Tennant) and Rose (Billie Piper).**

Above: **The Doctor (David Tennant) and Donna (Catherine Tate) in a scene from *The Runaway Bride*.**

Series Three (2007)

Smith & Jones

University of Glamorgan (Royal Hope Hospital interior) and Singleton Hospital, Swansea (exterior), Outside Blueberry Hotel and Grill, Market Street, Pontypridd (Jones family row), Queen Street, Cardiff (outside the Royal Hope), Quay Street, Cardiff (Martha on the phone)

The Shakespeare Code

Ford's Hospital, Greyfriar's Lane, Coventry (London streets), Cheylesmore Manor House, Coventry (street) Lord Leycester Hospital, Warwick - www.lordleycester.com (street), Shakespeare's Globe, London (The Globe Theatre), Blueberry Hotel and Grill, Pontypridd (Shakespeare's room), Newport Indoor Market (Bedlam)

Gridlock

Temple of Peace, Cardiff (New York Senate building), Ely Papermill, Cardiff (warehouses), The Maltings, Cardiff Bay (alley)

Daleks in Manhattan
Cogan playing fields, Penarth (Tardis lands), Pare and Dark Theatre, Treorchy (theatre), Trident Park, Cardiff Bay (Dalek Base), Bute Park, Cardiff (Central Park), Headlands School, Penarth (theatre backstage)

Evolution of the Daleks
See *Daleks in Manhattan*, plus: Treberfydd House, Llangasty, Brecon - www.treberfydd.com (Hooverville Guard)

The Lazarus Experiment
Wells Cathedral, Wells (Southwark Cathedral), Senedd Building, Welsh Assembly, Cardiff, (Lazarus Institute), Sir William House, Tresillian Terrace, Cardiff (Lazarus's office), National Museum of Wales, Cardiff (press conference), Biomedical Science Building, Cardiff University (laboratory)

Above: **Freema Agyeman as Martha Jones** *Below:* **Catherine Tate as Donna Noble in *Partners in Crime***

_42_
House in Cwrt-y-Vil Road, Penarth (Francine's House), Trident Park, Cardiff Bay (ship control panels), St Regis Paper Company mill, Caldicot (space ship)

Human Nature
Treberfydd House, Llangasty, Brecon - www.treberfydd.com (Farringham School), Llandaff, Cathedral, Cardiff (school dormitory and war memorial), Tredegar House, Newport (school), St Fagan's National Museum, Cardiff (village and dance hall)

The Family of Blood
See Human Nature, plus: Neal Soil Supplies Rumney, Cardiff (First World War battlefield)

Blink
Former NatWest Bank, Bute Street, Cardiff (police station), West Bute Street, Cardiff (outside the pub), Miners Hospital, Caerphilly (Welgrove Hospice), St Woolos Cemetery, Newport (Kathy's Grave), House at 18 Fields Park Avenue, Newport (Wester Drumlins), Alexandra Gardens, Cathays Park, Cardiff (site of staues), Chartist Tower, Newport (Billy meets the Doctor and Martha)

Utopia
Trident Park, Cardiff Bay (radiation room and corridors), Roald Dahl Plass, Cardiff (rift site), Argoed Quarry, Llanharry (surface of Malcassairo), Wenvoe Quarry, Wenvoe (rocket silo site)

The Sound of Drums
Fortes, Paget Road, Barry Island (café), Hensol Castle (Downing Street), Cwrt-y-Vil Road, Penarth (Francine's and Clive's homes), Maelfa Shopping Centre, Llanedeyrn, Cardiff (The Doctor and the Master talk), Wenallt Road, Caerphilly (hillside), RAF St Athan (airstrip), Whitmore Bay, Barry Island (timelord initiation), Penarth Esplanade (Martha warns Leo), University Place, Cardiff (outside Martha's flat). Other locations: The Friary, Cardiff, High Street, Penarth, Millennium Square, Cardiff.

Last of the Time Lords
See The Sound of Drums, plus: Vaynor Quarry, Merthyr Tydfil (the Doctor confronts the Master) , Whitmore Bay, Barry Island (Martha arrives), Roald Dahl Plass, Cardiff (farewell to Jack), Alexandra Gardens, Cardiff (Martha gives flowers). Also used: Aberthaw Power Station, Barry

Voyage of the Damned
Mamhilad Industrial Estate (Deck 31), The Coal Exchange, Cardiff Bay (Titanic lounge) Working Street, Cardiff (passengers teleport and London street), inside Exchange Building, Cambrian Place, Swansea (Titanic teleport)

Above: **The return of the Cyberman** *Below:* **You thought the Tardis just appears... two members of the Doctor Who team assemble the famous blue box on location.**

Partners in Crime
Helmont House, Churchill Way, Cardiff (Adispose Industries), Nant-Gawr Showcase Cinema, Pontypriddn (presentation), Toilets at Tiger, Tiger, Cardiff (toilets), Fat Cat Café, Greyfriars, Cardiff (café), Nant-Fawr Road, Cardiff (Donna's home), Charles Street, Cardiff

The Fires of Pompeii
Cinecittà Film Studios, Rome (private), Temple of Peace, Cardiff (Temple), Clearwell Caves, Gloucestershire (inside the volcano) Morlais Quarry, Merthyr Tydfil (Mount Vesuvius slopes)

Planet of the Ood
Lafarge Cement Barry (Ood compound), Trefil Quarry, Tredegar (Ood Sphere), Mamhilad Park Industrial Estate, Pontypool (warehouse)

The Sontaran Stratagem
Margam Country Park, Port Talbot (academy), Compass Bridge Road, Cardiff (car goes into water), Cargo Road (Atmos controls jeep), Mamhilad Park Industrial Estate, Pontypool (factory)

The Poison Sky
See *The Sontaran Stratagem*

The Doctor's Daughter
Newbridge Memo, Newbridge (human base), Plantasia Botanic Gardens, Swansea (the Source), Kenfig Hill, Bridgend (Messaline), Barry Shooting Range (bunker)

The Unicorn and the Wasp
Cefn Llwyd lake Caephilly (lake), St Senwyr's Church, Cowbridge (church), Hensol Castle - www.hensol.co.uk (The Harrogate Hotel), Llansannor Court (Edison Manor)

Opposite page: **Kylie Minogue takes a break from filming *Voyage of the Damned* in Swansea.**

2008 Christmas special
St Woolos Cemetary, Newport, Gloucester Cathedral, Miller's Green, Gloucester

Classic Doctor Who

In the 45 years since *Doctor Who* began, the time travelling Doctor has been all over the galaxy - without leaving Earth! Credit must go to the show's many location managers who, over the years, have managed to find dozens of British locations to play either far-off planets or Earth in the past, present or future. What follows are some of the more interesting locations used over the years for filming of the classic series of *Doctor Who* - but clearly it is not an exhaustive list.

The First Doctor - William Hartnell (1963-1966)

Back in 1964, when the late William Hartnell played the Doctor, the dreaded Daleks invade the planet in the story *The Dalek Invasion of Earth* and are seen roaming in London near the Houses of Parliament, in Trafalgar Square, on Westminster Bridge, on the South Bank, at Whitehall, at the Albert Memorial. The footage shot in Trafalgar Square was shot at 5am and was supposed to show deserted London where everyone was hiding away from the Daleks. It looked deserted - except that if you look very carefully you will see a bus! The 1966 story *The Smugglers* was filmed at Nanjizal Bay in Cornwall.

The Second Doctor - Patrick Troughton (1966-1969)

Doctor number two, played by the late Patrick Troughton, lands his Tardis at Gatwick Airport in the story *The Faceless Ones*. The Nant Ffrancon Pass and Ogwen Lake in Snowdonia, Wales, played a more exotic location: Tibet, home of the Yeti - or so it appeared - in the 1967 story *The Abominable Snowman*. But when the Yeti takes over the London underground in *The Web of Fear*, London Transport demanded so high a fee for the use of its tube tunnels - and then only in the early hours of the morning - that the BBC filmed most of the story on studio sets. Climping Beach, Littlehampton, West Sussex was used for *The Enemy of the World*. The series took to the sea - well, the Thames Estuary - for the 1968 story *Fury From The Deep*, filming on the Radio 390 Offshore Platform at Red Sands and on the beach at Kingsgate in Kent. One of the series' most visually spectacular location sequences came in the 1968 story *The Invasion* when a supposedly massive army of Cybermen sweeps into London. After emerging from sewers, the Cybermen were later seen descending the steps with St Paul's Cathedral in the background. The quarries seen in *The Krotons* were in Malvern, Worcestershire and a string of locations in West Sussex including Clayton and East and West Dean were used for *The War Games*.

Below: **Jon Pertwee on location in Portsmouth for the filming of *The Sea Devils.***

The Third Doctor - Jon Pertwee (1970-1974)

When the late Jon Pertwee took over the role of the Doctor in 1970 he came face to face in his first adventure with plastic monsters, the Autons, in *Spearhead from Space*. In another eerie sequence, the Autons, in the guise of tailors' dummies, came alive in a shop window, smashed their way out and started walking down the street shooting people. This scene was filmed early one Sunday morning in Ealing High Street in north London. The inside of Madame Tussaud's in London was also used for a scene. The story also called for scenes at a hospital and at the headquarters of the United Nations Intelligence Task Force (UNIT) - and these were shot at the BBC's Engineering Training Centre at Wood Norton, near Evesham. In the 1971 story *The Mind of Evil*, Dover Castle played a prison where the evil Master, played by Roger Delgado, is being kept under lock and key. During the story prisoners take over the prison and the authorities send in UNIT troops to storm it in one of the programme's finest action sequences. Later that year the Wiltshire village of Aldbourne played the fictional village of Devil's End in the popular story *The Daemons*. The village pub, The Blue Boar, doubled as The Cloven Hoof and the village church was used as the church. The barrow, which played Devil's Hump in the series, is about 1/4 of a mile from Aldbourne up a dirt track. Aldbourne was used for English village scenes in *Band of Brothers*. The 1972 story *The Sea Devils* used one of the most unusual locations - 19th Century No Man's Land Fort in the sea between Portsmouth and the Isle of Wight. The Royal Navy helped the BBC with *The Sea Devils* and allowed them to use its Whale Island base, HMS Excellent, in Portsmouth as the fictional HMS Seaspite, and also Frazer Gunnery Range. This time Norris Castle on the Isle of Wight was used as a prison for the dastardly villain, The Master. In the 1973 story *The Three Doctors*, Denham Manor, Denham, Buckinghamshire became UNIT headquarters and some footage of William Hartnell, who was too ill to film in London, was recorded in the garden of his home in Mayfield, Sussex. *The Time Warrior* was filmed at Peckforton Castle in Cheshire (see www.peckfortoncastle.co.uk) and *The Green Death* was filmed at a colliery, now Darran Valley country park in Deri, Glamorgan.

Above: **Sarah-Jane Smith (Elisabeth Sladen) tries to escape from Linx, a sontaran in *The Time Warrior***

The Fourth Doctor - Tom Baker (1975-1981)

Tom Baker's first story *Robot* was filmed at Wood Norton Hall in Worcestershire (see www.wnhall.co.uk) and other locations in his first season include: Hound Tor on Dartmoor (*The Sontaran Experiment*) and Wookey Hole caves at Wells in Somerset (*Revenge of the Cybermen*). Scotland was the setting for *The Terror Of The Zygons* but the BBC decided to film much of it in West Sussex. Among the key locations was a pub - The Fox Goes Free at Charlton. Athelhampton House, near Dorchester in Dorset, was the location for the 1976 adventure *The Seeds of Doom* and had also been used for *Sleuth* which stars Michael Caine and Laurence Olivier. Mick Jagger's former home, Stargroves, at East End near Newbury, was used in stories *The Pyramids Of Mars* and *The Image of The Fendahl*. Tom Baker's final scenes in *Logopolis* were filmed at BBC receiving station in Crowsley Park, Berkshire which played the Pharos Project.

The Fifth Doctor - Peter Davison (1982-1984)

Peter Davison, the fifth Doctor, filmed some of his first story *Castrovalva* at Harrison's Rock, Groombridge East Sussex, *The Visitation* at Black Park, near Fulmer in Buckinghamshire (also used for the Baker story *Full Circle*, the Sylvester McCoy story Battlefield as well as several *Harry Potter* films, the Bond film *Casino Royale* and *Batman*) and some of *Time-Flight* at Heathrow Airport. *Mawdryn Undead* was filmed at Middlesex University, Trent Park, Barnet, *The King's Demons* at Bodiam Castle, East Sussex, *The Awakening* at Shapwick in Dorset. Much of the 1984 story *The Resurrection of The Daleks* was filmed in Shad Thames in the London Docklands. Much of the 1983 20th Anniversary show, *The Five Doctors*, was filmed in North Wales (including at a quarry at Blaenau Ffestiniog), although one of Jon Pertwee's sequences in his car, Bessie, was filmed in Denham. Footage of Tom Baker, who didn't take part in the episode, was taken from the 1979 story *Shada*, which had never been finished because of a BBC strike. In the sequences, the Doctor and his assistant Romana, played by Lalla Ward, are seen punting on the river in Cambridge.

The Sixth Doctor - Colin Baker (1984-1986)

Sixth Doctor Colin Baker had to endure freezing temperatures when he filmed his only Dalek story, *Revelation of the Daleks*, in the snow at Butser Hill near Petersfield. IBM's then futuristic looking UK headquarters at North Harbour, Portsmouth, was used for later scenes also shot in the snow. Blists Hill Victorian Town in Shropshire was used in *The Mark of the Rani*. Camber Sands in East Sussex was used for *The Ultimate Foe* (and had also been used for *The Chase* and the films *Dunkirk* and *Carry On: Follow That Camel*.

The Seventh Doctor - Sylvester McCoy (1987-1989)

Seventh doctor Sylvester McCoy was supposed to film his 1988 story *Silver Nemesis* at Windsor Castle, but this was blocked by officials so the shoot was switched to Arundel Castle in West Sussex which played Windsor instead. In later scenes Greenwich Gas Works was used as a landing site for a Cyberfleet. Lulworth Cove in Dorset featured in *The Curse of Fenric* and Kew Bridge Steam Museum in Brentford (see www.kbsm.org) was used in *Remembrance of the Daleks*.

The Eighth Doctor – Paul McGann (1996)

Paul McGann made just one appearance as the eighth Doctor in the 1996 adventure *Enemy Within* which was filmed in Canada and San Francisco.

Gavin and Stacey

Barry

The gentle comedy series *Gavin and Stacey* has won millions of fans and has rightly garnered a string of awards since it began in 2007. It has also done much to put the Welsh town of Barry, a few miles from Cardiff, on the map. In the comedy, Stacey (Joanna Page) is from Barry and Gavin (Matthew Horne) is from Essex. But the difference in backgrounds and culture doesn't hinder their romance, which flourishes when they finally met after hitting it off during numerous flirtatious work calls.

Despite being supposedly set in Barry and Essex, location filming for the show is all done in and around Barry, a small town in the Vale of Glamorgan, South Wales. Stacey's house is a private residence on Trinity Street and Gavin's parents' home, supposedly in Billericay, Essex, is in Dinas Powys, the next settlement to Barry. Gavin and his mate Neil's (James Corden) local pub in Essex is actually the Colcot Arms, Colcot Road, Barry. The amusement arcade where Nessa (Ruth Jones) works is at The Western Shelter, Barry Island, Barry's coastal resort and when the family go on a bingo outing during series two those scenes were filmed at Penarth Pier. King's Square in the centre of Barry, outside the Town Hall, was the spot where Nessa decides to try to earn some money as a performance artist (*left*). Also featured regularly is Barry Town Station and the branch of Burger King where Gavin's sister works, again supposedly in Essex, is at Culverhouse Cross near Barry. "We're now having people phoning up saying that they are coming to stay in Barry because of *Gavin and Stacey*," said Tourism and Marketing Manager Claire Evans. "It is really putting us on the map."

The Prisoner

Portmeirion

The cult 1960s series *The Prisoner* was filmed at the privately owned Mediterranean-style village of Portmeirion in North Wales. The village, situated at the top of a wooded clifftop, on its own private peninsula overlooking the Traeth Bach estuary and Cardigan Bay, was the inspiration of architect Sir Clough Williams-Ellis who fell in love with the Italian fishing village of Portofino as a young man and resolved to one day create something as charming in Britain. In 1925 he bought a small craggy, wooded peninsula situated between Harlech and Porthmadog. Over the next few years he converted an early Victorian house on the site into a luxury hotel and added cottages. He travelled the country purchasing architecturally interesting but dilapidated buildings, set for demolition, which he brought to Portmeirion and rebuilt.

Above: **It looks like it could be Italy, but actually it's Portmeirion in Wales.**

The village, which became a popular place for visitors including Edward VIII, HG Wells, John Steinbeck and Noel Coward, who wrote his play *Blithe Spirit* while staying at the hotel, was completed in 1973 and now comprises 50 buildings arranged around a central piazza. Actor Patrick McGoohan discovered Portmeirion while filming an episode of his 60s spy series *Danger Man* in Wales. He realised it was the perfect location for a new series he'd been planning called *The Prisoner*, which showbiz mogul Lew Grade had agreed to finance with a then unheard-of budget of £75,000 an episode. The series follows the surreal adventures of an ex-spy with no name, just a number - Number Six - marooned in a strange village from which he constantly tries to escape. The 17-

part series was a massive hit attracting around 12 million viewers each week. Today the series enjoys cult status and members of The Prisoner Appreciation Society, Six of One, stage a yearly convention at Portmeirion where they re-enact episodes and play the famous Human Chess Game. Portmeirion is open all year round. The hotel was gutted by fire in 1981, but has now been completely renovated and is a splendid place to stay. It has also become a popular venue for weddings. For further information see www.portmeirion-village.com

Above: **Three views of Sir Clough Williams-Ellis' amazing creation, Portmeirion.**

Also in Wales

Edge of Darkness

The BBC thriller *Edge of Darkness* sees the late Bob Peck playing Yorkshire detective Ronald Craven who is investigating the death of his daughter Emma who'd been part of an ecology group which had discovered a secret nuclear plant Northmoor under the Welsh mountains. In reality Northmoor was created by set designers who built an underground complex inside a disused slate mine at Manod, Blaenau Ffestiniog. The entrance used by Craven and CIA officer Darius Jedburgh to enter Northmoor was actually shot at a gold mine at Dolgellau. Llechwedd Slate Caverns at Blaenau Ffestiniog are open to the public. For details telephone: (01766) 830306 or visit www.llechwedd-slate-caverns.co.uk The conference sequence in the last episode was filmed at Gleneagles in Scotland.

Our Mutual Friend

The Blitz combined with modern development caused a headache for the production team preparing to recreate 1860s London for the BBC's 1998 version of *Our Mutual Friend* which stars Paul McGann, Anna Friel, David Morrissey and Keeley Hawes. The major location was a sprawling warehouse on the riverfront overlooking the Thames at Southwark, but there was no genuine site which fitted the bill so a set was built at Cardiff Docks. Elsewhere, a disused stone quarry at Trifil, Wales was used and 17th Century Honington Hall, Shipston-on-Stour, Warwickshire, played Mr and Mrs Boffin's home after they gain their wealth. Scenes were also filmed all over London including the English Speaking Union in Charles Street, which played the Veneerings house, the Middle Temple, Lincoln's Inn Fields, Gun Street, Somerset House and the back streets scenes behind the warehouses were filmed at Chatham Dockyard.

The North West

Bread

Liverpool

Elswick Street used to be just another smart row of two-up, two down terraced houses just a few yards from the River Mersey in Liverpool. But all that changed when a BBC film crew arrived - and it ended up becoming one of the most famous streets in Britain. As the setting for the comedy series *Bread*, Elswick Street, became a popular place for tourists to visit. The big Boswell family lived at Number 30 on screen and grumpy Granddad lived next door at Number 28.

Bread's writer Carla Lane chose Elswick Street (*pictured left*) to appear in *Bread* because it fitted the image she had of where the Boswells lived and because the road ran down to the River Mersey it suited the scenes she planned to write.

When she writes a script Carla actually tells the location manager on the show where she thinks something should be filmed. "I go out on my own and look at places and then I write them in a script," she said. "Then the BBC go out and find them from there. I give them more than a hint - I tell them where!"

Brookside

Liverpool

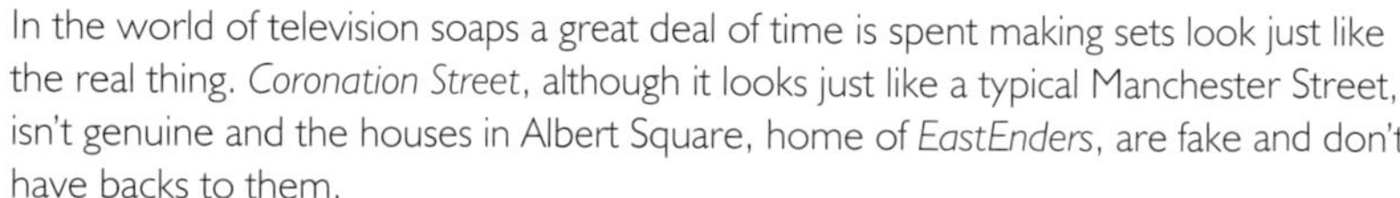

In the world of television soaps a great deal of time is spent making sets look just like the real thing. *Coronation Street*, although it looks just like a typical Manchester Street, isn't genuine and the houses in Albert Square, home of *EastEnders*, are fake and don't have backs to them.

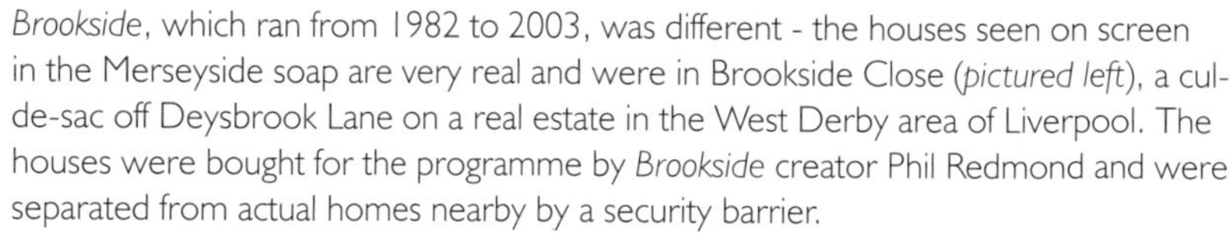

Brookside, which ran from 1982 to 2003, was different - the houses seen on screen in the Merseyside soap are very real and were in Brookside Close (*pictured left*), a cul-de-sac off Deysbrook Lane on a real estate in the West Derby area of Liverpool. The houses were bought for the programme by *Brookside* creator Phil Redmond and were separated from actual homes nearby by a security barrier.

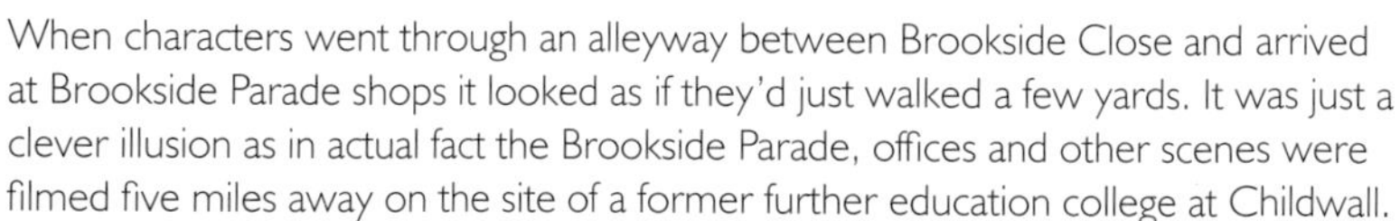

When characters went through an alleyway between Brookside Close and arrived at Brookside Parade shops it looked as if they'd just walked a few yards. It was just a clever illusion as in actual fact the Brookside Parade, offices and other scenes were filmed five miles away on the site of a former further education college at Childwall.

After the series ended the houses (the six that were seen on screen and seven which were used by the production team as offices) were set to be sold off in the spring of 2008. In March 2008 filming of a horror movie, *Salvage*, starring Shaun Dooley and Neve McIntosh, took place in the close.

Coronation Street

Manchester

Britain's longest-running soap first aired in 1960 and nearly 50 years later, is still going strong. Set in fictional Weatherfield, *The Street*, or *Corrie* as it is fondly known, is shot mainly on a set at Granada Television's studios in Manchester, although outside locations are also used from time to time. The original *Corrie* outside set was built in 1969, but prior to that point, everything had been filmed inside a studio. That exterior set was demolished in 1982 and the current one was built at the same time.

The soap's sets change and evolve to meet the needs of the storylines as well as technology. The first sets back in the 60s were long and thin because of fixed lens cameras. Now they can be designed as required; it's simply up to the designer's brief and imagination. As fans of the drama will know, the set incorporates regular fixtures: the Rover's Return pub, a corner shop, a row of terraced houses, two shop units, three houses and a factory – all built in the 80s. Since then, other features have been added from time to time, such as Leanne Battersby's Italian restaurant (recently burnt down), a betting shop and Audrey's hair salon, to name a few.

In 1988, the Granada Studios Tour was opened to the public and millions have had the opportunity to walk down the famous cobbles of *Coronation Street*. They were able to stand at the bar in the Rover's Return and peek into Rita's sweet shop. Unfortunately, Granada stopped offering tours in 1999. Some of the off-set locations used by *Corrie* over the years include the stunning Arley Hall and Gardens Estate near Northwich in Cheshire, one of the most interesting stately homes in the North West. Open to the public for corporate events and glamorous weddings, it has served as an ideal romantic venue for three Coronation Street weddings, as well as one for the BBC drama Cutting It.

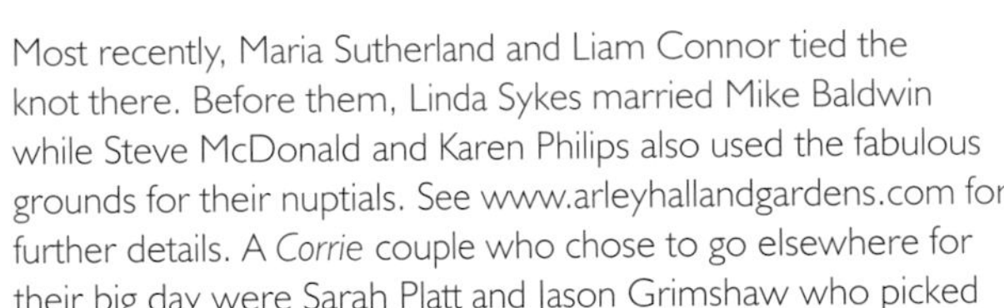

Most recently, Maria Sutherland and Liam Connor tied the knot there. Before them, Linda Sykes married Mike Baldwin while Steve McDonald and Karen Philips also used the fabulous grounds for their nuptials. See www.arleyhallandgardens.com for further details. A *Corrie* couple who chose to go elsewhere for their big day were Sarah Platt and Jason Grimshaw who picked the attractive Ryecroft Hall in Audenshaw instead. Dating back to the 19th Century, the hall was originally built for a wealthy family but it is now Audenshaw's community centre. Other Corrie weddings and funerals have been filmed at a church in Prestwich to which the production returns frequently.

Above: **One of the most recognisable sights in Britain...*Coronation Street.***

One of *Coronation Street's* biggest storylines involved the deadly Richard Hillman who met a watery death in 2003 after driving himself and his family into a canal. This was shot at the Portland Basin Museum, Portland Place, Ashton under Lyne. Actor Brian Capron who played Hillman went on to win a Soap Award for Best Exit later the same year.

Life on Mars

Stockport

The first series of *Life on Mars* was screened by the BBC in 2006 and became an instant hit with viewers, going on to win both an Emmy and a BAFTA. Thanks to its quirky storyline and top notch cast – notably John Simm and Philip Glennister – it quickly developed a cult following which has remained loyal, despite only one more series being made the following year. It tells the story of DCI Sam Tyler, played by Simm, an officer with the Greater Manchester Police who wakes up in 1973 after being hit by a car. He finds himself working for Manchester and Salford police force as a DI with a new boss, the maverick DCI Gene Hunt (Glenister).

Described as a 'science-fiction cop drama,' viewers are left wondering whether Tyler is dreaming his new life or whether he really has travelled back in time. Originally, the series was going to be shot in London which then changed to Leeds. Two months before filming began it was settled – Manchester was the chosen location. Tuning in every week while the show was still on air, it was fun for millions to recognise various landmarks in and around Manchester, Bury, Oldham, Salford and Stockport. Fans of *Life on Mars* love to work out where particular episodes were shot and there are several websites dedicated to location spotting.

Below: **Philip Glenister, Liz White and John Simm in a break during filming of *Life on Mars*.**

The police station used by the A Division CID team was actually the back of Stopford House, the home of Stockport Council Offices on Piccadilly. With its close proximity

to the M60, the A6 and the centre of Manchester it makes sense that it was chosen by the location team to double up as the now iconic cop shop so closely associated with *Life on Mars*.

"It was actually built in 1971 so it fitted perfectly with what we were trying to achieve," said Location Manager Brett Wilson who worked on series one. "We were making out it was the new Manchester police headquarters which in 1973 when *Life on Mars* is set, it would have been." Behind the council building is Stopford Piazza which also features heavily in the show revamped as a 70s police station car park, complete with Cortinas, bicycles and lampposts. Most of the interior scenes such as the main CID office were shot on a purpose-built set at the BBC's studios in Manchester.

The spot where modern day Sam is hit by a car in the first episode was filmed in a service road underneath the Mancunian Way in Manchester, just off the A6 London Road heading towards Stockport.

The other two main places frequently revisited in *Life on Mars* are Sam's dingy gaffe and the pub, both of which were specially created sets, but fans have always been quick to recognise a whole host of other locations which have proved vital to the success of the show.

"We filmed lots of different scenes at the Rochdale Canal at Ancoats," Brett continued. "The opening sequence when Sam comes round in 1973 and is found by a policeman at the car crash site was shot on some waste ground. We also shot the arrest of the villains bursting out of the swimming baths and running along the canal in their trunks by there in another episode." The Grade II listed Victoria Baths in Hathersage Road, Manchester were used in filming at least two episodes. The 100-year-old building was used by the public until 1993 and is renowned for its exquisite architecture, stained glass and ornate tiling. It is currently undergoing restoration works after winning the BBC's *Restoration* series. The red bricked boiler house complex at the back of the building became the old waterworks in one episode and was used in the second series as a warehouse. The Turkish Baths within the same complex doubled up as the morgue in series two with its Victorian tiling perfect for the purpose.

"We used a real morgue in the first series, at St Thomas's Hospital in Stockport," Brett said. "But it got sold to developers so we had to find another one and the Turkish Baths doubled up perfectly and looked very convincing." Victoria Baths are open to the public on the first Sunday of every month between March and October and on National Heritage Days, September 11-14. Telephone 0161 224 2020 for further information or go to www.victoriabaths.org.uk

Many of the industrial back streets used in *Life on Mars* were just off Great Ancoat Street in the Ancoats district, Pollard Street East and Upper Cyrus Street. With its high redbrick walls and run down character, the area was perfect for many of the walking, talking scenes. Mills at Chadderton near Oldham were also used for some exterior shots with interiors filmed at a museum, Queen Street Mill in Burnley.

"The residential roads were a mixture of all sorts," Brett continued. "We used roads in Gorton, Rusholme and Levenshulme to name a few areas. And in Gorton we found

Above (top): **John Simm as Sam Tyler** *(middle)* **Philip Glenister and John Simm take a break** *(bottom)* **The scene of Sam's accident.**

an old derelict house which was gutted and due for renovation which we dressed accordingly and used for some interior shots. The Rainbow Cafe, again in Ancoats, was used a couple of times. In series one there was a robbery at a mill that had gone wrong and someone went to pick some guns up from the cafe. We used the same cafe for a police meeting during a heist at a newspaper office in another episode."

Woodgate Street and Eustace Street in Great Lever, Bolton, which still boast great cobbles, were used extensively for series two including for a brass band car chase. Brett admitted it's not easy filming a period show in Manchester but is full of praise for the local authorities who welcome production companies into the area. "You have to find vistas which don't take in the cityscape," he explained. "They've got to be contained so you've got to have high buildings around you which are period and don't give the game away. It was difficult but there's a wealth of stuff in Manchester to use; you just have to do the leg work and put in the hours to find it."

Below: **Marshall Lancaster (DC Chris Skelton), Liz White (WPC Annie Cartwright) and Philip Glenister (DCI Gene Hunt) on location.**

Pride and Prejudice

Lyme Park

Jane Austen's comedy of manners *Pride and Prejudice* caused a sensation when it was screened on the BBC in September and October 1995 and turned its two lead actors Colin Firth, who plays Mr Darcy, and Jennifer Ehle, who plays Elizabeth Bennet, into stars. The story centres on Mrs Bennet, played by Alison Steadman, and her pursuit of husbands for her five daughters from the eligible rich young men who come into their social world in 19th Century Hertfordshire.

The BBC's previous version, adapted by Fay Weldon and screened in 1980, had been studio based but the six-part 1995 adaptation, written by award-winning screenwriter Andrew Davies, featured some of Britain's most stunning houses and countryside. For the purposes of filming, Mr Darcy's stunning home Pemberley is quite a distance from Derbyshire, where it is supposed to be, and its exterior shots were actually filmed at beautiful Lyme Park in Cheshire.

Lyme Park, one of the largest houses in the county, is owned by The National Trust and was the home of the Legh family for 600 years. It is open to the public most of the year. Interior shots of Pemberley were actually filmed closer to where they were set, at late 17th Century Sudbury Hall in Derbyshire, which is again owned by The National Trust. Go to www.nationaltrust.org.uk for details.

Right: **Colin Firth and Jennifer Ehle as Mr Darcy and Elizabeth Bennet in the 1995 BBC adaptation of *Pride and Prejudice*.**

The Bennet family home Longbourn was actually Luckington Court near Chipping Sodbury in Wiltshire. The house is privately owned and a popular wedding reception venue but is not otherwise open to the public. For further details see www.luckingtoncourt.co.uk

Just 15 miles away is the beautiful village of Lacock, which is also owned by The National Trust, and played Meryton on screen. The village dates back to the 13th Century and its limewashed half-timbered and stone houses also featured in *Harry Potter*, the ITV dramatisations of *Moll Flanders*, *Emma* and *Cranford*.

The production team filming *Moll Flanders* reportedly managed to upset the locals by using tonnes of soil to cover up the modern tarmac. Torrential rain later the same day then washed several inches of mud all down the main street.

"Even though Lacock is a very pretty place there were still scores of things we had to do to dress it properly," said Gerry Scott, Production Designer on *Pride and Prejudice*. "Contemporary shop fronts had to be covered or altered, many of the doors were covered with modern-day gloss paint and others had the wrong type of knocker or bell-push. "We had to go to the people who lived there and say 'Look, do you mind if...?' and without exception everyone was very kind and allowed us to tinker with their property."

The Ballroom at Brocket Hall, at Welwyn, Hertfordshire, was used for the main ball held at Netherfield. The Ballroom at Brocket Hall, which is now an upmarket conference venue, is 60 feet long and cost a then exorbitant £1,500 when it was first furnished back in 1760. For details see the Brocket Hall website at www.brocket-hall.co.uk The other scenes at Netherfield were filmed at Edgecote Hall near Banbury in Oxfordshire but this is privately owned and not open to the public. Rosings, home of Lady Catherine was played by Belton House at Grantham, Lincolnshire.

Above: **Stunning Lyme Park, one of the largest stately homes in Britain was the main locatation for *Pride and Prejudice*.**

Belton, which was built in the late 17th Century, is also now owned by The National Trust and is open for much of the year. For further details go to www.national-trust.org.uk Other scenes were filmed outside the Lord Leycester Hospital in Warwick and the Lambton Inn was in Chapel Street, Longnor, Staffordshire. Jane Austen's real house is now a museum and is located in the village of Chawton near Alton in Hampshire. For details see www.jane-austens-house-museum.org.uk. The writer's grave can be found in Winchester Cathedral.

The North

All Creatures Great and Small

Askrigg

All Creatures Great and Small was one of the BBC's biggest drama hits of the 70s and 80s. Based on the novels of vet James Herriot, the series stars Christopher Timothy as Herriot and Robert Hardy as his partner Siegfried Farnon. The real-life surgery on which the books were based is in Thirsk, but the BBC used pretty Askrigg to play fictional Darrowby. Clearly visible in the village is tall Skeldale House which played the vets' surgery. Next door is a Sykes Store, which played a sweet shop in the series and across the road is Sticky Ginger café, which was used as the grocer's shop. Nearby is The King's Arms, which played The Drover's Arms. Not far from Askrigg is Bolton Castle, where James proposes to Helen. It was also used in the BBC series *Ivanhoe* and the feature film *Elizabeth*. (see www.boltoncastle.co.uk) Other locations used in the series include: the market in Hawes, which played Darrowby Cattle Market, Hardraw church which was Darrowby church and Wensley church, where James and Helen are married.

Right: **James Herriot (Christopher Timothy) and Siegfried Farnon (Robert Hardy) the stars of *All Creatures Great Small.***

Born and Bred

Downham

Stunning scenery helped make *Born and Bred* compelling Sunday night viewing between 2002 and 2005. Set in the fictional Lancashire village of Ormston during the 50s, it centres on the relationship between village GP Arthur Gilder (James Bolam) and his city-trained doctor son Tom Gilder, played by Michael French. Much of the family drama was filmed in the real-life village of Downham, near Clitheroe in Lancashire. The village is privately-owned by Lord and Lady Clitheroe and every home is rented by the villagers. What made it the perfect location for a 50s-set series such as this is the fact that certain trappings of modern day life are banned making it not too dissimilar to the way it was centuries ago. Ormston Hospital was actually the exterior of three houses within the village.

Right: **The pretty village of Downham played Ormston in the popular series BBC *Born and Bred***

Brideshead Revisited

Castle Howard

When it was first screened the worldwide success of the ITV epic drama *Brideshead Revisited* brought thousands of extra visitors flocking to the series' principal location, Castle Howard in Yorkshire. And even now, two decades after the series was shown in Britain, it still contributes heavily to the number of visitors to Castle Howard, which has been the seat of the Howard family for more than three centuries. *Brideshead Revisited* is often cited as one of ITV's biggest successes - both critically and in terms of ratings - but filming didn't run smoothly. It cost Granada, who made it, more than twice the original budget and a strike by television workers held production up and the crew was disbanded at one point.

When the series finally went into production Granada managed to find a distinguished cast including Laurence Olivier, John Gielgud, Anthony Andrews and Jeremy Irons. The tale of love and passion during the inter-war years was filmed against a backdrop of 18th Century Castle Howard, one of the finest stately homes in Britain, which is set in 1,000 acres of parkland and is as stunning on the outside as it is beautiful inside.

Castle Howard is no stranger to filmmakers. In 1965 it featured in the film *Lady L* which starred David Niven, Sophia Loren and Paul Newman and it also featured in a BBC version of *Twelfth Night* in 1978 and in 1994 the BBC returned to film the costume drama *The Buccaneers*. In the summer of 2007 a new version of *Brideshead Revisited* went into production starring Michael Gambon and Emma Thompson and much of it was also filmed at Castle Howard. For more details and opening times see www.castlehoward.co.uk

Below: **The splendour of Castle Howard, the location for *Brideshead Revisted.***

Emmerdale

Esholt

There's good news and bad news for fans of the ITV soap *Emmerdale*. First the good news, you can visit both villages originally used as Beckindale in the series. The bad news is that you can no longer visit the exterior locations for the show since filming was switched from the village of Esholt to a specially built set on an estate in North Yorkshire in January 1998.

The pretty village of Arncliffe played the first Beckindale but production was moved in 1976 because producers decided to find somewhere closer to Leeds, where the interior scenes are recorded, because it was quite a trek to Arncliffe. Not only that, Arncliffe had become a Mecca for fans and the village just couldn't cope. Filming was switched to Esholt, just a few miles north west of Leeds, and that in turn became a magnet for lovers of the show, so much so that a special parking site for coaches had to be built nearby.

Then in 1997 Yorkshire Television decided to build a purpose built set on the estate which surrounds historic Harewood House near Leeds, which was once used for the ITV series *Follyfoot*. The success of the series and the pressures of extra episodes made shooting at Esholt too difficult. It had been fine when they only made one episode a week but new episodes heavily increased the workload.

Below: **It looks real - but the *Emmerdale* pictured here is a specially-built set.**

The new set, which took four months to build, isn't an exact replica and Yorkshire Television received quite a few letters when it was first seen on screen because some viewers noticed the change, despite the efforts of expert painters and carpenters.

Unfortunately the set isn't open to the public and a few years ago Yorkshire Television stopped its popular tours of interior sets that it used to run at its Leeds studios. A small consolation is that you can watch a live webcam of the location set. Go to www.itv.com/soaps/emmerdale/webcam/default.html

Not every location is on the Harewood Estate set. Creskeld Hall at Arthington doubles as Home Farm and has seen plenty of drama over the years including Frank Tate's death, the murder of Tom King, Zoe blowing up part of the house and Tom being pushed out of his bedroom window. It is now the longest serving location on the programme.

However, Esholt is still worth a visit. As you drive into the village you'll pass the coach park on the left. If you take the next left you'll find yourselves in Main Street and halfway down on the left is The

Woolpack pub, with a car park behind. The pub, which used to be called The Commercial until the name was changed to fit in with the show and attract tourists, was only ever used in the series for exterior shots.

"The inside of our pub isn't the same as people see on screen and it is funny seeing their faces when they come in for the first time," said landlady Nicki McGrath, who runs the pub with her husband Richard. "But they still get a warm welcome. It is quite amusing seeing the outside of 'our pub' on screen – and trying to spot little differences. The *Emmerdale* connection is still good for business and we still get a lot of coach parties coming here."

A few yards down Main Street, also on the left, is the village hall, which has featured extensively in the series. Just opposite the hall is St Paul's Church which played Beckindale Church, where Matt married Dolly, Kathy married Jackie and Joe married twice in the show.

Above: (left): **The real Woolpack in Esholt** *(centre)* **the entrance to the television set village** *(right)* **the television Woolpack.**

Out the other side of the church is The Vicarage, which was home for many years to Reverend Donald Hinton, but which in real life has now been turned into three homes. Turning left at the end of Church Lane, follow Chapel Lane for a short while until you find Cunliffe Lane.

Turn into it and you'll see Bunker's Hill, which was better known on screen as Demdyke, until it was 'destroyed' on screen in the 1993 plane crash storyline. On screen, Number Six played Seth Armstrong's house and Number Three used to house Nick, Elsa and Alice. And - just a reminder - the houses are homes to real people not connected with *Emmerdale*.

Market scenes have been filmed in the nearby town of Otley, which plays Hotten in the series and other places that have been used include: Almscliffe Crag, Brimham Rocks, Plumptom Rocks, Valley Gardens, Harrogate and Golden Acre Park, Leeds. In addition Wakefield, Leeds and Morley town halls have been used for courtroom scenes.

Emmerdale's title sequence shows off some of Yorkshire's finest countryside including Ripon, Ramsgill, Gouthwaite and Eccup reservoir, Pateley Bridge and Blayshaw Aquaduct.

Heartbeat

Goathland

The picturesque North Yorkshire village of Goathland has always been a popular place for tourists due to its superb views of the moors. Being used as the setting for Yorkshire Television's drama *Heartbeat* was guaranteed to bring a host of new visitors to the village. At the start of the series former *EastEnders* actor Nick Berry played London police constable Nick Rowan who quit his inner city beat to take a job as a rural village bobby along with his doctor wife Kate, who was played by Niamh Cusack.

The series, which is set in the 60s, follows Nick and Kate's lives from the moment they move into the Aidensfield police house. Inevitably, over the many years the series has been running, members of the cast have changed and these days it is PC Joe Mason (Joe McFadden) who pounds the rural beat along with PC Don Wetherby (Rupert Ward-Lewis).

Former policeman Oscar Blaketon (Derek Fowlds) now runs the village pub, The Aidensfield Arms along with Gina Bellamy (Tricia Penrose) and the series remains as

Below: **PC Rob Walker (Jonathan Kerrigan), district nurse Carol Cassidy (Lisa Kay) and PC Phil Bellamy (Mark Jordon).**

Above (left): **Glendale House, which was used as Kate Rowan's surgery and is now a B&B** *(right)* **Gina Ward (Tricia Penrose) and David Stockwell (David Lonsdale).**

popular as ever so much so that it has now been running longer than the actual 60s themselves.

There's plenty to see in Goathland for *Heartbeat* fans and when you drive through the village you'll reach a right-hand bend and the stone house on your right is Glendale House, which played Kate Rowan's surgery in the series. The house was built in 1875 by Edward Fuller Sewell, an uncle of Anna Sewell, author of the novel *Black Beauty*.

It's a Victorian stone-built residence and occupies a prime position in the centre of the picturesque village, overlooking the common, where sheep graze right outside the garden gate. Its owners, Keith and Sandra Simmonds, offer reasonably priced bed and breakfast. For details see www.glendalehouse.co.uk

Sandra says the impact of *Heartbeat* on Goathland has been positive. "*Heartbeat* has been very good for business and the production team have bent over backwards to minimise disruption to the village," she said. "We've had visitors from as far afield as Tasmania, Russia and even Peru because of *Heartbeat*."

Over at Brow House Farm, which used to be used as the location for Claude Greengrass' farm, farmers John and Keith Jackson have opened up some of their fields as a campsite. "We had the site up and running before *Heartbeat* began but now people know the series is filmed here they are keener than ever to come and stay," said Keith. In fact business has been so good recently that the Jacksons have given another field over to campers to cope with demand.

"Business has picked up a lot," he said. "And so we opened the other field up because we couldn't get them all on the original site. It seems the more popular *Heartbeat* gets, the busier we are - there's no doubt about that." Facilities offered to campers and caravanners include running water, a shower and toilets and electricity hook-up points. Bookings can be made by telephoning 01947 896274.

Real life Goathland Garage appears in the series as Scripp's Garage and across the road from it is The Goathland Hotel which plays the local pub, The Aidensfield Arms. You'll also see the shops which feature in the series including the real post office which plays the post office in the show and Aidensfield Stores, run by Phil and Ros Hopkinson, which remains the same on the outside whether filming is taking place or not and sells a range of *Heartbeat* merchandise. See www.aidensfieldstores.co.uk for further details. "*Heartbeat* has been great for business," said Phil. "And the show's popularity internationally means we get people here from all over the world."

The Goathland Primary School featured heavily in the show when Nick Rowan's second wife Jo Weston was in the series and in real life the school benefited from a donation from Yorkshire Television which helped kit the pupils out in new school uniforms. A private house, Brereton Cottage on Brereton Corner now plays the police house and also not open to the public is a farm which plays Peggy Armstrong and David Stockwell's farm.

We don't often see the exterior of the police station on screen these days, but in older episodes the former police station in Courthouse Street, Otley, about 75 miles from Goathland, was used. When *Heartbeat* began most scenes – both interior and exterior - were filmed in Goathland but now most interior scenes are shot at a studio built inside a former mill near Leeds, which was once used as the studio for filming interiors for *Emmerdale*. Sets of Ashfordly Police Station, the doctor's surgery and the pub have been built there as it is cheaper and easier to film interior scenes there.

Below (left): **Tricia Penrose (Gina Ward) and Derek Fowlds (Oscar Blaketon) film a scene on location in Goathland** *(right)* **Members of the crew 'create' a police station**.

Above: **A view of picturesque Goathland.**

Jane Eyre

Bakewell

An all-star cast helped make BBC's 2006 glossy adaptation of Charlotte Bronte's *Jane Eyre* one of the most popular television remakes of this much-loved classic, winning both an Emmy and a BAFTA the following year. It had previously been filmed by the BBC 13 years earlier when a future James Bond – Timothy Dalton – was cast as Rochester and an unknown actress, Zelah Clarke, played Jane.

ITV had its own version in 1997 with Samantha Morton in the title role and Ciaran Hinds as Rochester. The BBC's 2006 four-part serial features relative newcomer Ruth Wilson as Jane and Toby Stephenson as the brooding Rochester, with the likes of Pam Ferris as Grace Poole, Francesca Annis as Lady Ingram and Tara Fitzgerald as Mrs Reed.

Dovedale, the rocky National Trust land in the Derbyshire Dales, is featured in the opening episode of the BBC's 2006 version where Rochester and Jane initially meet in the mist. Rochester's home, Thornfield, was in fact Haddon Hall, a stunning medieval castle in Bakewell, Derbyshire which is owned by Lord and Lady Edward Manners. Some of the scenes supposedly set at Thornfield were in fact shot at a studio miles away and at another building.

Haddon Hall has featured in a number of other television shows and films, including the BBC's *The Prince and the Pauper* and more recently, the movie remake of *Pride and Prejudice*, starring Keira Knightley and Matthew MacFadyen. In particularly dramatic scenes, Thornfield is seen burning through the night, thanks to the use of special effects. During filming the local fire brigade received dozens of calls from worried locals who believed Haddon Hall was genuinely on fire. For further information go to www.haddonhall.co.uk If you're planning on visiting Bakewell, why not take in the village of Hathersage in Derbyshire which is just eight miles drive north. Once renowned for its milling industries, the area is now the perfect place to walk and climb as it is overlooked by moors and gritstone edges, including the well-known Stanage Edge. Ruth Wilson's Jane is seen standing here in episode four.

Charlotte Bronte visited Hathersage in 1845 and took the name Eyre for her novel's heroine from the local family. It is believed that she based Thornfield, the house from where Mrs Rochester jumps from the roof to her death, on North Lees Hall, an Elizabethan manor house which is situated about a mile north of Hathersage. In the book she describes it as: "three storeys high, of proportions not vast, though considerable: a gentleman's manor house." This description fits North Lees Hall to a tee. The BBC certainly thought so and used the Hall as Thornfield (along with Haddon Hall as mentioned earlier). The property is now owned by the Peak District National Park Authority and is open to the public for one weekend in September. Telephone Yorkshire Bridge Inn Ltd for further information on 01433 651361.

If you stood on Carhead Rocks above North Lees Hall and looked behind you, you'd see Overstones Farm, which doubled as Rivers Cottage. "Much of the Peak District, particularly the land around Overstones Farm is perfect for filming purposes because it's remote and utterly timeless," said local photographer Stephen Elliott.

Below: **Ilam Park, one of the settings for *Jane Eyre*.**

Above: **Beautiful Dovedale in the Derbyshire Dales.**

Much of the early part of Jane Eyre takes place at Lowood School and for this, the BBC opted for Bolsover Castle which provided some of the school's interiors. Built in the 12th Century, it is now in the care of English Heritage. It also served as Jane's school during her early years when she was played by the young actress Georgie Henley, while some of her fellow pupils were played by youngsters from local drama school, the Ripley Academy. The Riding House at Bolsover Castle was transformed into the school's dormitory. Wingfield Manor at South Wingfield, near Alfreton, Derbyshire was used as Thornfield after the great fire had wreaked havoc. A ruined country mansion, it was once the home of one of Britain's wealthiest men, Lord Ralph Cromwell, having built it for himself in 1439. It's particularly fascinating when you learn that Mary Queen of Scots was held prisoner here three times in the 1500s. The building has remained unoccupied since 1772 and is now owned by English Heritage To arrange to visit or learn more about its history see www.english-heritage.org.uk.

Ilam Hall at Ashbourne, a 19th Century Victorian Gothic manor house, and its surrounding gardens are managed by the National Trust and are now used as a youth hostel, tea rooms and car park. The hall doubled up as the exterior of Lowood School. Situated in the village of Ilam, it is to be found between Buxton and Ashbourne. Tel 0870 7705876 to book the youth hostel. For more details about the house see www.nationaltrust.org.uk Another Trust property, Kedleston Hall, an 18th Century mansion north-west of Derby, featured in the scene where Rochester meets his future wife Bertha. The mansion is renowned for its art treasures and one particular room, Caesar's Hall, was transformed into a Caribbean setting where a lavish dinner was staged. Go to www.nationaltrust.org.uk to learn more about this stunning building and for details of opening times.

Last of the Summer Wine

Holmfirth

Roy Clarke's gentle comedy *Last of the Summer Wine* has given the Yorkshire town of Holmfirth the sort of publicity that tourism industry chiefs usually can only dream of. Since it began more than 30 years ago the series has put the town firmly on the tourist map and shown off the full beauty of the Pennine countryside. Each year thousands of fans of the BBC comedy flock to Holmfirth to see for themselves the real-life setting for the show. In the olden days it was the haunts of Compo, Foggy and Clegg that drew the crowds, but over the years, as older cast members died or retired, a new set of equally eccentric but loveable characters have been brought in and have blended seamlessly with the gentle spirit of the show and its their town people want to explore.

A good first port of call in Holmfirth - particularly after a long drive - must be the cafe used as Sid's Cafe in the series, now run on-screen by Ivy. A former paint store for a nearby hardware shop, the cafe looks much the same off screen as on and the BBC, who have always used the outside for filming, now sometimes use the inside as well.

Local man Colin Frost ran the cafe with his wife Maggie for 15 years until 2006 when it was taken over by sisters Ailsa and Laura Booth. "The popularity of *Last of the Summer Wine* goes right round the world," said Ailsa. "We've had customers from as far afield as Australia and New Zealand and even people from Finland," she said. The café is open for most of the year except when filming takes place and sells a range of merchandise including mugs, tea pots, t-shirt and fridge magnets.

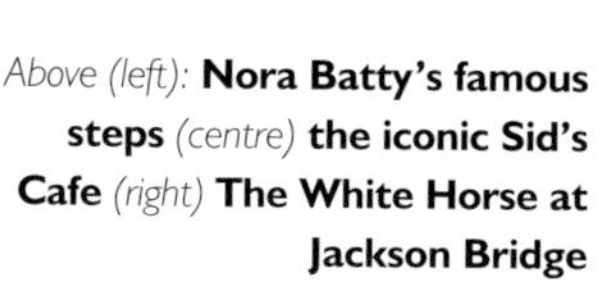

Above (left): **Nora Batty's famous steps** *(centre)* **the iconic Sid's Cafe** *(right)* **The White Horse at Jackson Bridge**

Former owner Colin Frost now runs tours of filming locations. See www.summerwine.tv for details. No trip to Holmfirth is complete without taking a peek at Nora Batty's famous house. It is just a short walk from the cafe along Hollowgate. At the end of Hollowgate is a bridge and from it you can see Nora's house, Number 28 Scarfold and below is the door to Compo's flat, which now houses The Summerwine Exhibition, run by Sue and Chris Gardner. The couple also own The Wrinkled Stocking Tea Room next door at Number 30, another good place to take a break. It is open for most of the year. See www.wrinkledstocking.co.uk for details.

Nora's house is now available as a holiday cottage and if you stay there then you could be lucky and find the BBC crew filming on your doorstep. Businessman Neil Worthington bought the house a few years ago and planned to expand his graphic design and advertising business at Numbers 24 and 26 into it. But he changed his mind and decided to open the world-famous house for self-catering accommodation instead. For booking details see: www.nora-batty.co.uk

"99.9 per cent of people who stay are fans of the show and I think they quite like the idea that they might wake up one morning and find cameras outside ready to film a scene," said Neil.

The house even contains some Nora Batty props and as Neil's website says it is "A shrine to Nora Batty, fully furnished, as only Nora would approve. Tastefully decorated in keeping with the overall Nora Batty Experience." Neil added: "We're quite unique – there aren't many film sets you can actually stay in."

While in the area you might like to call in for a pint at The White Horse Inn at Jackson Bridge which has appeared in the show many times. See www.thewhitehorsejacksonbridge.co.uk for details. Behind the pub at Jackson Bridge is the private house which doubles as home for Cleggy, Pearl and Howard. From Jackson Bridge you may like to drive to Hepworth where you'll find another of the trio's locals, The Butcher's Arms. See www.butchersarmshepworth.co.uk for details.

Left: **Nora Batty dishes out justice to Compo, Foggy and Clegg.**

Open All Hours

Doncaster

You won't find Arkwright's grocers shop open all hours if you go to Number 15, Lister Avenue in Doncaster. Nor will you be able to buy a p-p-p-packet of cornflakes or a l-l-l-loaf of bread. But you might be able to get your hair cut! For the shop that played stuttering Arkwright's shop in the highly successful BBC comedy *Open All Hours*, and became Britain's best-known shop front, is actually a hair salon.

The BBC picked the shop because it had a traditional double front and fitted the bill perfectly as Arkwright's old-style corner shop. So for three weeks a year, for four years, the BBC rolled their camera equipment into the street and moved owner Helen Ibbotson's hairdryers and curlers out of her shop. The BBC covered up Helen's Beautique sign with a board bearing Arkwright's name and dressed up the front of the shop with stocks of food. And, of course, they painted details of Arkwright's bargain of the week on the window.

"It was never a real inconvenience," Helen explained. "I used to shut down when they were here. The BBC used to pay me very nicely - a bit more than the hairdressing. So it paid for a holiday, which was very handy." Helen got another bonus too - free vegetables!

After filming had ended the BBC often used to give her Arkwright's vegetables. "They gave me a lot of the stuff and I made wine with the parsnips and carrots," she said. Helen had good memories of the show's two stars Ronnie Barker, who plays stuttering Arkwright, and David Jason, who plays Granville. She said: "David was a very funny man and nice to get on with. Ronnie was very nice too but a bit more serious than David - but still very jolly. People seemed to like them in the street. They always used to get a good crowd when they were filming."

Above (left): **Ronnie Barker and David Jason as Arkwright and Granville on location in Doncaster** *(right)* **the shop as it is now.**

Across the road from Helen's shop is Number 34 which played the home of Arkwright's love, nurse Gladys Emmanuel (Lynda Baron). After it was used for the first series the then owner altered the look of the front of the house and when the BBC came to make the next series they decided it no longer suited them. So filming was switched to Number 32 next door - and the BBC hoped no one would notice. In 2006 Doncaster council chiefs put forward a new development plan for parts of the town which many people believed could see areas including Lister Avenue facing demolition. A petition and campaign have been set up against the plan, although councillors accused campaigners of scaremongering and said nothing had been finalised.

The Royal

Scarborough

Heartbeat spin-off *The Royal* is filmed in the seaside town of Scarborough and centres around the fictional St Aiden's Royal Free Hospital. Exterior shots for the series, which stars Robert Daws as Dr Gordon Ormerod and Amy Robbins as Dr Jill Weatherill, are shot outside Red Court apartments in Holbeck Road.

Interior scenes are filmed in a studio, but other locations that have been used for the series, include Goathland and Calverley. Scarborough has been featured many times on TV and in films with appearances in *Little Voice*, *Rik Mayall Presents: Dancing Queen* and *Dalziel and Pascoe*.

Wire in the Blood

Newcastle

This long-running crime series which was first screened on ITV in 2002, has proved hugely successful and is sold to over 30 countries around the world. Made by Coastal Productions *Wire in the Blood* is filmed in and around Newcastle and stars Robson Green as clinical psychologist Dr Tony Hill who gets inside the head of killers in order to help police solve bizarre crimes.

He works closely on a range of often gruesome cases with Detective Inspector Alex Fielding, played by Simone Lahbib who took over in series four from Detective Chief Inspector Carol Jordan, played by Hermione Norris.

Newcastle itself is never mentioned in *Wire in the Blood* which is supposedly based in the fictional metropolis of Bradfield. "This is taken to be 'somewhere up north,' and is very definitely not Newcastle, or anywhere else for that matter," said Location Manager Gareth Williams. "In fact we have some night aerial shots which were taken over Birmingham just because looking down from a helicopter over Birmingham at night with all the twinkling lights, looks good.

"We have studiously avoided anything that readily identifies the city as Newcastle. We think that's important because Coastal have always avoided postcard drama. The

Below: **The city of Newcastle is used as the setting for *Wire In The Blood.***

city has got loads of wonderful locations but we don't want people to visually tire of the north east. We just want *Wire in the Blood* to be applauded for its general artistic creative merits rather than where it happens to be."

As fans of the drama will know, it is a dark show and as much of it is filmed during the winter, when there is plenty of darkness to give it the look the producers are after. A large part of *Wire in the Blood* is filmed on a purpose-built set, home to the police station, which is currently flat packed awaiting filming to begin at a warehouse in Heaven, Newcastle. For the first three seasons, the inside of the police station was filmed in the former Bank of England in the centre of Newcastle. The building has an interesting history – it was the second biggest bullion store in the country outside of London – but the set itself wasn't felt to be especially interesting.

The current set used for *Wire in the Blood* began to take shape in series four when the production team came across a former Rolls Royce switch gear factory on the Team Valley. With its ranks of grey steel shelving and steel staircases, it was considered ideal police station material.

Said Gareth: "We changed the colour of the floor to a dark aquamarine blue, we rearranged the shelving a little bit, brought in some oversized furniture to match the oversized space we were in and had manufactured some steel grill panels that we could move around and put in front of the camera to shoot through. Hey presto, a police station set."

Unfortunately, after series four, the building wasn't available any longer so Gareth bought all of the steel staircases and grey shelving which were moved to another warehouse in Wallsend, Newcastle. The designer for series five remodelled the set using the props and made it even more camera friendly. That was the blueprint for the set used for series six, although in the interim, the production lost the warehouse. Early in 2008, Gareth was sent to find a similar warehouse and managed to track one down in Heaven which is where the set is now standing, getting dusty and waiting to be reused.

As fans of *Wire in the Blood* will know all too well, the drama is a very sombre one and old, derelict buildings are often perfect for the storylines. Gareth's job is to hunt out disused buildings such as old churches and schools which are on the turn. Indeed, he says over the past six years he has often bumped into Newcastle's police sniffer dog training unit because they have the same interests – semi-derelict properties.

"It's too expensive to use a decent building, take out the furniture and repaint it to look derelict," he said. "I need to find buildings that are like that already although it can't be too dilapidated in case it's dangerous.

"Newcastle has a wealth of locations which we've been able to use over the years although it's a city in transition which means the locations we used in the early series, are probably no longer around anymore."

Scotland

Doctor Finlay

Auchtermuchty,

Auchtermuchty became the fictional Scottish town of Tannochbrae in the 1993 series of *Doctor Finlay* by chance when the series' producer Peter Wolfes drove through the town on his way to view another possible location. Many buildings in the town centre,The Cross, were used for filming and The Forest Hills Hotel became a temperance hotel, The Salvation. The Post Office appeared regularly although it was turned into The Flying Dutchman pub.

Auchtermuchty Town Hall, which was the town's police station many years ago and still has the old cells, reverted back to its former role to play Tannochbrae Police Station. The town's council offices doubled as the local bank and the entrance to the library was altered to fit the 1950s style and was used as Tannochbrae library. What was missing from Auchtermuchty, of course, was the surgery, Arden House, and that was because it wasn't in the town. In fact it was more than 70 miles away on a country estate just outside Glasgow. The original 60s series *Doctor Finlay's Casebook* was filmed in Callander but producers decided not to use it for the 1993 series because it had become too busy.

Hamish MacBeth

Plockton

The sleepy village of Plockton on the north west coast of Scotland found fame in the late 1990s as the fictional village of Lochdubh, home beat of PC Hamish Macbeth, played by Robert Carlyle, who has gone on to become a major film star. To find the right location to play Lochdubh for the BBC series, the show's producers toured 1,200 miles of the west coast of Scotland. "As soon as we saw Plockton we knew it was perfect," recalled Producer Deidre Keir. "It's extraordinarily beautiful, it's not on a main road and it has the same kind of close-knit community as Lochdubh."

Although remote, Plockton (*pictured left*) is just over the sea from Skye and attracts visitors from all over the world. It lies in a sheltered inlet, surrounded by heather-clad mountains and with views across Loch Carron, the gulf stream climate accounts for unexpected palm trees which fringe its harbour and seals are a common sight in its calm waters. Before the BBC team arrived in the village enmasse Deirdre and her team made sure the locals were happy with the prospect of a 70-strong film unit arriving. Plockton's newsagent Edmund McKenzie agreed to move his shop into the sailing club next door for three months so that his premises could be used by the BBC and converted into the Lochdubh general store. Visitors to Plockton were constantly surprised to find the village shop was faked and stocked only with props. The whitewashed house chosen to be both Hamish's home and the police station is a holiday home owned by a Glasgow doctor. On one occasion a family from London who had pre-booked a week's holiday arrived to find their cottage adorned with a blue lamp and bars at the window and police cell where a bedroom used to be.

High Road

Luss

The Scottish soap, which ran from 1980 to 2003, was filmed in Luss on the banks of Loch Lomond where the pretty village doubled as fictional Glendarroch. The big house in the series was actually the Youth Hostel at nearby Arden, which can be seen from the main road and the hostel's annexe nearby played the Glendarroch Hotel in a series, although the interior shots were recorded in the studio. Anyone wanting to stay at the hostel must be a member of the Youth Hostel Association.

In Luss (*pictured left*) itself, filming took place at the Highland Arts Gift Shop, which played Blair's Store, outside several cottages, at the church and at the manse. The ferry used to feature regularly and we often saw characters walking along the beach and on the pier. A farm at nearby Glenfruin was also featured. The nearby town of Helensburgh also appeared in the series for lots of shop scenes and the Coffee Club in Colquhoun Square appeared regularly.

Monarch of the Glen

Loch Laggan

Thanks to its views of the glorious Scottish Highlands and acres of breathtaking scenery, *Monarch of the Glen* became unmissable Sunday night viewing between 2000 and 2005, with seven successful series making it one of the most popular television shows to come out of Scotland.

Even now, it is repeated all over the world and fans still make their way to stunning Loch Laggan, 16 miles south west of Newtonmore where much of the series was filmed, to catch a glimpse of all the landmarks which made *Monarch* so memorable.

The gorgeous setting for the fictional village of Glenbogle, with its mixture of eccentric and somehow innocent characters, is the village of Laggan and the splendid Glenbogle Castle, inhabited by Richard Briers' character Laird Hector Bogle, was played by the privately-owned Ardverikie House. The house can be seen – and photographed – from across the loch on the main Newtonmore to Fort William Road and indeed, many fans of the show still visit Ardverikie when they're in the area, despite it being off-limits to the general public.

"We always know where *Monarch* is showing at a given time depending on the nationality of our visitors," said Robert Noble who currently manages the Ardverikie House estate. "We get lots of Australian tourists for example and Norwegians. It's always being repeated somewhere. We can't stop people wandering on to the estate but we do

Right: **Privately-owned Ardverikie House, which was used as Glenbogle Castle in *Monarch of the Glen*.**

ask that they respect the privacy of the family and others who live here." During its heyday, *Monarch* brought a buzz to Ardverikie and Laggan as endless crew and cast members arrived to begin filming for several months at a time.

Laggan locals and residents from a little further afield in the Badenoch areas of Newtonmore, Kingussie and Kincraig and further still, Strathspey (the area from Aviemore northwards), which were areas also used to shoot scenes, often became extras, boosting morale no end and ensured everyone was happy with the whole *Monarch of the Glen* experience.

"The production company (Ecosse) were given exclusive rights to the main part of Ardverikie House between February and October each year in order to film Monarch," Robert continued. The family were able to use a wing during this period which had been renovated for them; then they moved back into the house once the film crews had left.

"It was obviously a very busy time while filming was taking place because there were about a 100 cast and crew and this of course meant it was very good for the local economy. They had to have accommodation and as there wasn't enough room on the estate for everyone, the local guest houses did very well. Again the local shops were very pleased of the extra custom too as were the pubs. All in all, *Monarch* was very good for the area and surrounding locations."

The Gate Lodge, a holiday cottage belonging to the estate was often featured on *Monarch*. With its turret and picturesque setting at the entrance to the grounds, it is an ideal honeymoon retreat and is nearly always booked up months, if not years ahead. Another larger, self-catering estate property, Gallovie, doubled up as a bed and break-

Above: **Richard Briers, Alastair Mackenzie and Susan Hampshire, the stars of *Monarch of the Glen.***

fast in the final series of Monarch. Again, it is possible to stay here – if you're lucky enough to book early. There are also a further three self-catering properties available to rent on the Ardverikie estate. For further information, go to www.ardverikie.com

The loch itself also became a feature of *Monarch*. A plane was sunk in its waters in one episode and of course, tragically Hector drowned in it. Susan Hampshire's character Molly was an artist and you may be interested to learning 'her' paintings were actually creations of a Newtonmore artist, David Fallows.

Local hotels often doubled up as Glenbogle premises and have become popular tourist spots as a result. For example, The Glen Hotel in Newtonmore, the car park of which sometimes popped up in *Monarch* is worth a visit. Go to www.theglenhotel.co.uk to make a booking.

As an impressive seven series were filmed in all, it's not surprising that a vast number of locations featured in *Monarch*, certainly too many to mention here, although the main ones have been highlighted. For further details go to www.monarchcountry.com

Taggart

Glasgow

This popular police drama from Scotland has been running for an incredible 25 years – so far – and has the honour of being the longest running detective drama on television anywhere in the world!

The late Mark McManus starred as DCI Jim Taggart in the pilot episode screened in 1983 and he continued in the role as the tough, experienced cop until he passed away in 1994.

Taggart's young and relatively inexperienced side-kick was DS Peter Livingstone, played by Neil Duncan, while his boss, Superintendent Jack McVitie was played by Iain Anderson. In 1987, Mike Jardine (James MacPherson) joined the show and four years later, Jackie Reid – Blythe Duff – replaced Livingstone as Taggart's right-hand officer.

It was a severe shock to the whole cast and crew when Mark McManus died suddenly in the middle of filming and his absence had to be explained away in the script. Jardine had already been elevated to DI and he was joined by his own side-kick, DC Stuart Fraser, played by Colin McCredie. DI Robbie Ross played by John Michie joined the team in 1998.

In 2002, actor Alex Norton's character DCI Matt Burke replaced Mike Jardine (who was killed off when MacPherson decided to leave) so today, Norton, McCredie, Michie and Duff are the four current stars of the show which celebrates its 25th anniversary in 2008.

Above: **The late Mark McManus, the original star of *Taggart*.**

Taggart is filmed primarily in the Glasgow area, although as you can imagine, in its quarter of a century, literally hundreds of locations have been used so it would be a near impossible task to try and list each and every one of them here!

But certainly when you tune in, it's possible to instantly spot some well-known attractions such as the famous St Andrews Suspension Bridge which is located in the corner of Glasgow Green, furthest from the City Centre. The Bridge links Glasgow Green with St Adelphi Street on the other side of The Clyde.

Then there's Central Station, Glasgow's main railway station; The People's Palace which was built in 1898 as a cultural centre for the city's workers; The Winter Gardens, a large conservatory on the back of the Palace; Glasgow School of Art; George Square; Barrowland where a street market takes place every week; Scott Street, Buchanan Street and a string of restaurants and cafes.

Exterior scenes for the police station are filmed at the Colville Building, North Portland Street, which is part of Strathclyde University. The main police station and incident room featured in every episode are actually purpose-built sets and these have been constructed in around a dozen or so locations since *Taggart* began.

"We've had one place for a few years then another one becomes available so we have to be on our toes and move on. The principal interior has changed quite a lot over the course of the series," explains Location Manager Donald Mackinnon who has worked on several episodes. "At the moment we're using an industrial unit at Polmadie."

Over the years, the use of new technology has crept on to the set and now plasma screens and some computer generated graphics are all part of making *Taggart* a 21st Century police drama.

"We film pretty much all around Glasgow; we use the city as a backdrop and have evolved alongside it," said Donald. "We feature the university quite a lot, the West End, many of the city's shipyards and of course the river as a lot of people have been bumped off and later found there!

"We've had a few funerals as well. About six years ago when one of our major characters (Jardine) was killed off, he was buried at the Necropolis which is one of the most famous cemeteries in Glasgow."

In fact the Necropolis is part of Glasgow's 'Heritage Trail,' and is one of the most significant cemeteries in Europe, attracting visitors from all over the UK and abroad. Donald said: "Not so long ago we shot part of an episode in a little fishing village in Ayreshire called Dunure, which isn't actually that far afield for us.

"The challenge is trying to find places to film that look different but are actually not that far away. The good thing about *Taggart* is that it has a cache which opens a lot of doors for us. People know the show so well and are very familiar with it so they're very happy to help us. It is also the one show that has consistently shown the city of Glasgow evolve."

Jersey, Ireland and Northern Ireland

Bergerac

Jersey

For an island just nine miles long, with a population of just 83,000, there were an awful lot of crimes committed on Jersey during the 1980s - well on screen at least. But far from putting visitors off the success of the BBC detective series *Bergerac* brought visitors flocking to the island. The Jersey tourist authorities were delighted by the free publicity and they even hired the series' star, John Nettles, who played Triumph Roadster-driving Sergeant Jim Bergerac, to appear in their advertisements.

Most of the 45 square-mile island got a look in at some point during the series' 10-year run, which began in 1981. Lots of the locations used for the series are easy to see but not even a super-sleuth like Jim Bergerac could find the attractive stone cottage and farm that played his home in the first few series. For it was located in Queen's Valley in the east of the island and is now under hundreds of thousands of gallons of water as the whole valley was flooded in 1992 to make the new Queen's Valley Reservoir.

Above: **A young John Nettles as Jim Bergerac.**

Jim's ex-father-in-law, millionaire Charlie Hungerford, played by Terrance Alexander, lived in a luxury home, portrayed by two different houses. The first was Noirmont Manor, a beautiful house overlooking Belcroute Bay. The second was Windward House, which is private, and overlooks St Brelade's Bay. The Jersey Police Headquarters Jim works from, the Bureau Des Estranges (Department for non Residents) was supposed to be in St Helier but was actually, Haute de la Garenne, a former childrens' home in the Parish of St Martin's in the east of the Island, which the BBC also used as a production base during filming. In reality, there is no such police department. Haute de la Garenne, now a youth hostel, became the focus of a major police investigation in early 2008.

One of Jim's regular contacts was Diamante Lil, played by actress Mela White, who runs a restaurant and bar called The Royal Barge. In real life the restaurant is The Old Court House at St Aubin, a popular venue for both locals and visitors. Only the exterior was used for filming - the interior of The Royal Barge was a set built inside the Forum cinema in St Helier. Around the island dozens of places were used for filming the series. For example, the Round Tower, the most southerly German wartime fortification at Noirmont Point was used for an action sequence when a stunt man was thrown from the top of the tower to the rocks below after a fight.

The Norman Church of St Brelade, which dates back to the 11th Century, and its churchyard were used many times for weddings and funerals and the church hall played the headquarters of a dastardly medium in one episode. St Ouen's Manor, a private house which dates back to the 13th Century, was used repeatedly in the series in various guises as an art gallery and museum, as a French chateau, as the headquarters of a neo-fascist and as home to an eccentric millionaire, who is robbed by the ice maiden, Philippa Vale, played by Liza Goddard.

Beau Port, an attractive secluded beach, was featured in an episode where Charlie Hungerford plans to build a huge hotel complex on the valley leading to it and cover

Above: **Two views of the stunning island of Jersey**

the whole bay with a retractable glass dome. Needless to say, like many of Charlie's wilder ideas, it doesn't happen, on or off screen. Mount Orgueil Castle was used just once in *Bergerac* in an episode about a German film star, played by Warren Clarke, who was making a movie in Jersey about the wartime German occupation. Jim later has a fight with the character and that took place on a large German bunker on the southern headland at St Ouen's Bay.

The beach at St Ouen's was featured many times and in one episode two young surfers find the body of a skin-diver there. Not far away, at St Mary's, on the road from St Ouen to Trinity, is the Ecole Elementaire, which played the school of Jim's daughter Kim. John Nettles ran into trouble with the real Jersey police during the filming of one episode when Jim chases a villain across St Brelade's Bay on a jet ski. Afterwards he was ticked off by an angry officer.

Like viewers, John Nettles fell in love with Jersey while filming *Bergerac*, and used to have a home there. He has his own idea as to why the series was so popular. "It was very nice for people in the middle of an English winter to switch on the television to see lovely scenery, sunlit bays and all the rest of those things," he recalled.

"And what is nice about Jersey is that, even though it's only nine by five miles, it contains many locations. You might think you are in California if you are down at St Ouen's Beach with the sand dunes behind you and if you go to the north of the Island around Sorel Point you could think that you were in Cornwall, with the grey cliffs, small coves and great beaches."

"Therefore we could exploit that and we could get a camera crew around very quickly to very different locations. Most people who come across to the island are quite surprised to find out how small it is, because when we were filming we made it look much larger."

Ballykissangel

Avoca

Of course, the town of Avoca, in County Wicklow, which doubled on screen as the sleepy village of *Ballykissangel*, is actually in the Republic of Ireland and therefore obviously not part of Britain. It's included in this book simply because of the popularity of the BBC series and because it is within easy reach of the UK. The series began in 1996 and sees rookie English priest Father Peter Clifford, played by Stephen Tompkinson, arrive to take on a new job as the local curate. He becomes friends with local bar owner Assumpta, played by Dervla Kirwan, and soon wises up to the ways of the locals.

He faces ongoing battles with his immediate superior, wily old priest Father MacAnally, played by Niall Toiban, and local businessman Brian Quigley, played by Tony Doyle. After two series both Stephen and Dervla decided to quit the show and two new characters Orla O'Connell, played by Victoria Smurfit and Sean Dillon, played by Lorcan Cranitch, were introduced to fill the gap and the series remained popular.

Above: (left) **Assumpta Fitzgerald (Dervla Kirwan) outside Fitzgerald's** *(centre)* **The bridge on Avoca** *(right)* **Father Peter Clifford (Stephen Tompkinson) in thoughtful mood** *Opposite page:* **Assumpta and Father Peter in a scene from the popular series**

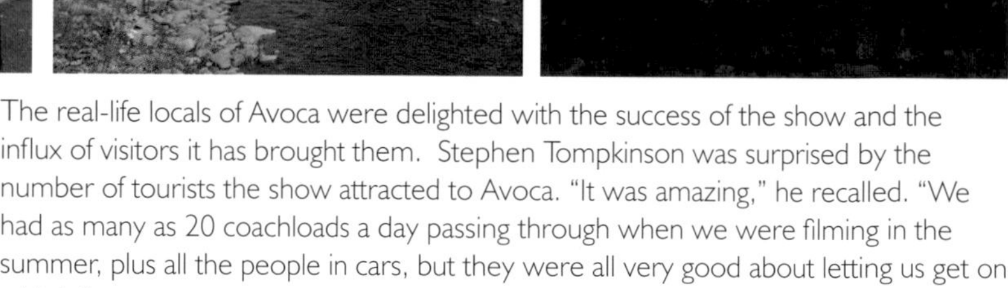

The real-life locals of Avoca were delighted with the success of the show and the influx of visitors it has brought them. Stephen Tompkinson was surprised by the number of tourists the show attracted to Avoca. "It was amazing," he recalled. "We had as many as 20 coachloads a day passing through when we were filming in the summer, plus all the people in cars, but they were all very good about letting us get on with it."

Most interior scenes for *Ballykissangel*, apart from Hendley's shop, which you can visit and has a fish and chip shop next door, were filmed in studios near Dublin but there's still plenty to see in Avoca. First stop might be Fitzgerald's, which played Fitzgerald's on screen (the name was changed for filming and the owners decided to stick with it) and where you're bound to get a warm welcome. About 100 yards up the road is St Mary and St Patrick Church, which doubled as St Joseph's. Then there is the local chemist which was used as the Post Office for filming. The locations for Quigley's House and Father Mac's were actually in Enniskerry, about 30 miles away. For more details see www.avoca.com and www.wicklow.ie

The Invisibles

Portaferry

Anyone heading to Devon in England to find the pretty seaside village which plays home to semi-retired criminals Syd Woolsey and Maurice Riley in the BBC series *The Invisibles* will be wasting their time. That's because although the series, which stars Warren Clarke, Anthony Head, Jenny Agutter and Dean Lennox Kelly is set in the West Country, it was actually filmed in Portaferry in Northern Ireland which doubles as Bidmouth.

The Northern Ireland authorities and the Irish Republican government (where some other scenes were filmed) offer tax breaks to film and television producers so it was decided to film *The Invisibles* there. To make sure it looked like Devon set designers hid any obviously giveaway that it was in fact Northern Ireland and dressed the set with Devon miscellany like posters.

Acknowledgements

The authors are indebted to all those who helped with the preparation of this book especially: (alphabetically): Simon Allen, Heather Armitage, Ralph Assheton, Kevin Bell, Jenny Bradley, Richard Brown, Joseph Cairns, James Caterer, Nicola Cheriton-Sutton, Nicola Clark, Andrea Collitt, Rikke Dakin, Harvey Edgington, Thomas Elgood, Jenny Ellenger, Stephen Elliott, Claire Evans, Pat Eyre, Midge Ferguson, Fiona Frankham, John Friend Newman, Chris Fulcher, Robbie Gibbs, Tryphena Greenwood, Dee Gregson, Mark Grimwade, Paul Gulliver, Javis Gurr, Arron Hendy, David Hitchcock, Andi Hollingsworth, Kerry Ixer, Christina Joyce, Stacey Killon, Jamie Lengyel, Caroline Lowsley-Williams, Jamie Lovelace, Alice Lumley, Donald Mackinnon, Nick Marshall, Natalie Moore, Michael More-Molyneaux, Hayley Morgan, Jess Newbould, Catriona Newman, John Friend Newman, Karen Nicholson, Robert Noble, Adrian Notter, Michele Notter, Emily Ogden, Frances Pardell, Katherine Powley, Keith Righton, Theresa Robson, Helen Saunders, Keith Simmonds, Sandra Simmonds, Andrew Sharpe, Lady Angela Stucley, Tony Tarran, Gillian Thompson, Chris Tinsley, Sarah Upton, Paul Vigay, Jenni Wagstaffe, Pete Ware, Rick Weston, Pam White, Gareth Williams, Brett Wilson and Stuart Wright.

The authors are also grateful to the photographers who kindly allowed their pictures to be used. They are credited below:

Picture credits

Jacket: Mark Campbell/Rex Features (Life on Mars); Martin Black/TV Times//www.scopefeatures.com (Doctor Who/David Tennant); TV Times/www.scopefeatures.com (Midsomer Murders); Brian Moody/ www.scopefeatures.com (Only Fools and Horses); ITV/Rex Features (Doc Martin); David Betteridge www.dhbphotography.co.uk (Cranford); Eagle Eyes (Little Britain); www.walesnews.com (Doctor Who/Billie Piper) page 2-3 www.dragon-pictures.com; page 9: Steve Clark; page 10: www.burnham-on-sea.com; page 11: Martine van Meerbeeck; pages 13-16: David Betteridge www.dhbphotography.co.uk; pages 17 & 18: Steve Clark; page 19: Courtesy of Alan Davies www.bigaldavies.co.uk; page 20: Rex Features; page 21-23: Chavenage; page 25: Steve Clark; page 26: Steve Clark • www.solentnews.biz • www.scopefeatures.com; page 27: South West News Service (SWNS); page 28: SWNS • Rick Weston; page 29: SWNS; pages 30 & 31: Courtesy of Owen Benson www.owenbenson.co.uk; page 32: © English Heritage Photo Library; page 33: Lady Stucley; page 34: Loseley House; pages 36-37: Mark Bourdillon / www.warnerleisurehotels.co.uk; page 38: ITV/Rex Features • Steve Clark; page 39: Bob Mazzer www.bobmazzer.com; page 40: Courtesy of Caitlin Ferguson-Mir www.photoexpedition.co.uk; 41: Eagle Eyes; page 42: ITV/Rex Features • Mark Emerson; page 43: ITV/Rex Features; page 44: Rex Features • Mark Fanthorpe; page 45: Bob Mazzer; pages 46 & 47: Bob Mazzer • Justin Lycett / Hastings Observer; page 49: Rex Features; page 50: Tony Larkin/Rex Features; page 51: Courtesy of Chester Tugwell; page 52: Tony Larkin/Rex Features; page 53: Courtesy of Loseley Park; page 55: ITV/Rex Features; page 56: © English Heritage Photo Library; page 57: Courtesy of Its Lefty • David Purton www.pictures4partners.co.uk / St Albans Register Office; page 58 & 59: Courtesy of Adrian Porter www.Ymzala.net; page 60: The News, Portsmouth; page 61 & 63: Eagle Eyes; page 65: Courtesy of the BBC; page 66: Dorset Echo; page 67: Courtesy of the Royal Oak • Courtesy of Jamie Barras; page 68: Eagle Eyes; page 70: Courtesy of Jamie Barras; page 71: Eagle Eyes; page 72: Courtesy of Lynford Hall Hotel • Edward Wing/Rex Features; page 73: Courtesy of Stuart Wright/The Dad's Army Appreciation Society; pages 74 & 75; Nick Ford www.nickpix.co.uk; pages 76 & 77: Eagle Eyes; page 78: Albanpix Ltd/Rex Features • Steve Clark; Page 79: © NTPL / Ray Hallett; Page 80: Courtesy of Michael J Davis; Pages 81 & 89: Courtesy of Kingpin Media; page 82: Rockingham Castle; page 83: www.shakespeare-country.co.uk; pages 84 & 86: Courtesy of www.britainonview.com; page 85: ITV/Rex Features; Page 87: Steve Poole / Scope Features; page 90: Minke Spiro/Rex Features • Lincolnshire County Council; page 91: © Andrew Tryner / Source: English Heritage Photo Library • ITV/Rex Features; page 92: © NTPL / Rupert Truman; page 93: www.walesnews.com; page 94: www.dragon-pictures.com; pages: 95 & 96; www.walesnews.com; pages 97 and 101: www.dragon-pictures.com; pages 98 & 100: www.walesnews.com; page 99: www.walesnews.com • www.dragon-pictures.com; page 102: The News, Portsmouth; page 103: Allan Ballard / www.scopefeatures.com; page 104: Courtesy of Darren Griffiths; page 105 & 106: www.portmeirion-village.com; page 107: Mark Campbell/Rex Features; page 108: Liverpool Film Office • Courtesy of Steve Drewry; Page 109: ITV/Rex Features; Page 110 & 112: www.cavendish-press.co.uk; page 111: www.cavendish-press.co.uk •Courtesy of Joseph Cairns; page 113: TVTimes/www.scopefeatures.com; page 114: © NTPL / Matthew Antrobus; page 115: Courtesy of Keith Simmonds www.glendalehouse.co.uk; page 116: Rex Features • Ribble Valley Borough Council; page 117: Castle Howard; page 118: Courtesy of Karen Lewis; page 119: Courtesy of Karen Lewis • Courtesy of Tim Green; page 120-123: Courtesy of Keith Simmonds www.glendalehouse.co.uk; page 124: © NTPL / Andrew Butler; page 125: © NTPL / Joe Cornish; page 126: Kirklees Council • Joyce Turner; page 127: Rex Features; page 128: Helen Ibbotson • Richard Brown; page 129: Newcastle City Council; pages 131, 133-134: www.visitscotland.com; page 132: Courtesy of Barbara Jones; page 135: Brian Moody / Scope Features; page 136: www.scopefeatures.com; pages137 & 139: www.jersey.com; page 138: Chris Craymer / www.scopefeatures.com; page 140: World Productions Ltd / BBC Photo Library • Chris Hill / www.discoverireland.com; page 141: World Productions Ltd / BBC Photo Library

Selected references & useful further reading

Bergerac's Jersey by John Nettles (BBC Books, 1988), The Bill - The Inside Story of British Television's Most Successful Police Series by Tony Lynch (Boxtree, 1991), Doctor Who magazine, The Only Fools and Horses Story by Steve Clark (BBC Books, 1998), The World of Inspector Morse by Christopher Bird (Boxtree, 1998), The World of Jonathan Creek by Steve Clark (BBC Books, 1999) and www.doctorwholocations.net

The authors would be pleased to hear from readers with details of new locations and updates on existing ones. Please contact them at locations@splendidbooks.co.uk or via the address on page 6.

Index